HOW TO
LEGALLY CHANGE
YOUR NAME
WITHOUT A
LAWYER. (Revised Edition)

LAW
AND
PRACTICE

THE NATIONAL LEGAL NAME CHANGE KIT

by
Benji O. Anosike, B.B.A., M.A., Ph.D.
Copyright, © 1991, 1998, by Benji O. Anosike.

Printing History:
First Edition, Oct. 1991
Second Edition, completely revised, June 1998

Library of Congress Cataloging-in-Publication Data

Anosike, Benji O.
    How to legally change your name without a lawyer : the national
legal name change kit / by Benji O. Anosike. -- 2nd ed., completely
rev.
        p.   cm.
    Includes bibliographical references and index.
    ISBN 0-932704-45-X
    1. Names, Personal--Law and legislation--United States--Popular
works.   I. Title.
    KF468.Z9A56   1998
    346.7301'2--dc21

D1262201

Printed in the United States of America

ISBN: 0-932704-45-X

Library of Congress Catalog Card No.:

Published by:
Do-It-Yourself Legal Publishers
60 Park Place
Newark, NJ 07102

ACKNOWLEDGMENTS

The author gratefully acknowledges the following people for their support and creative contributions:

Ms. Norma Feld, reference librarian, for her generous provision of access to the rich facilities of the Benjamin Cardoza Law School Library, New York; the editors and publishers of the Lawyers' Cooperative Publishing Co., publishers of the excellent <u>American Jurisprudence and Practice Forms</u> on name changing; and **Susan Deller Ross**, Professor of Law, Georgetown University Law Center and a leader in women's rights law development, for the invaluable strength and encouragement drawn from her professions of moral support and well-wishes in regard to this undertaking.

A very special thanks should go to **Professor Edward J. Bander** of the Suffolk University Law School (retired), author of the pioneering 1973 work, <u>Change of Name and Law of Names</u>, who, while engaged in lectures and in work for the Massachusetts Continuing Legal Education project and as editor of the Bi-Monthly Review of Law Books, somehow still found some precious time to review this publication and generously offer the benefit of his learned professional knowledge and critique on the contents thereof.

Finally, a most special thanks and fatherly well-wishes is reserved for the bouncing young fellow, **ODERAH EZIAFAKA ANOSIKE,** my brand new son of a few months of age!! His birth and youthful liveliness has brought new energy of spirit just at the nick of time while engaged in the research and writing of this work.

To all of the above, suffice it to say, simply, that you have in one special way or the other, by your words, acts or expressions, prior deeds, pioneering works and/or research in the field - and your unselfish readiness to share and disseminate the fruits thereof - made the present undertaking both more purposeful and easier for the present author.

Dedication

This Book is Lovingly Dedicated to...

Oderah Eziafaka Anosike

...for making life all too refreshing and re-invigorating all over again for your daddy!

The Publisher's Disclaimer

It remains for us, the Publishers, to assure our readers that we have diligently researched, checked and counterchecked every bit of information contained in this manual to ensure its accuracy and up-to-dateness. Nevertheless, we humans have never been noted for out infallibility, no matter how hard the effort! Furthermore, details of laws, rules, or procedures do change from time to time. And, with specific respect to name-changing and the like, the specific details of the rules and procedures that govern them (though generally not the law or the broad basic principles themselves) often differ from one state to another. Nor is this relatively short manual conceivable intended to be an encyclopedia on the subject containing the answer or solution to every issue on the subject. **THE READER IS THEREFORE FOREWARNED THAT THIS MANUAL IS SOLD AND DISTRIBUTED WITH THIS DISCLAIMER:** The publisher (and/or the author) does not make any guarantees of any kind whatsoever or purport to engage in rendering professional or legal service, or to substitute for a lawyer, an accountant, financial or social advisor, or the like. Where such professional help is legitimately called for in your specific or other cases, it should be sought accordingly.

--Do-It-Yourself Legal Publishers

TABLE OF CONTENTS

APPENDICES

LIST OF SAMPLE FORMS CITED IN THIS MANUAL
(Where to Find Them)

FOREWORD:

THE PUBLISHER'S MESSAGE

To All Our Dear Readers:

Take heart, folks. This is one subject matter where almost every key player in the game - the lawyer, the non-lawyer, the judge, and "the law" itself - is in uniform agreement that the use of a lawyer or even the courts to undertake it, is primarily unnecessary. California attorney and author **David Brown's** account on the matter probably sums up the often heard comment or expressed feeling across the board, in as well as out of the legal and judicial circles:

> "The law regarding name change is a rare Oasis in the vast desert of lawyers, courts, and judges. If ever there was any area of law where a lawyer is almost never required, this is it…Many Americans don't realize that changing a name is so easy. In deed, there is a common misconception that lawyers and courts must be involved in some mysterious mumbo-jumbo in order for…(one) to choose a new name. But the simple fact is that (that is absolutely not the case)"*

HOW TO LEGALLY CHANGE YOUR NAME WITHOUT A LAWYER, in a word, seeks at long last, to give you, the reader, precisely those tools and knowledge you'd need to be able to translate the much vaunted ideal of a simplified non-lawyer, non-expensive legal name change world into actual reality.

Here is, at once, your tool to exercise and reclaim your American birth right to adopt a name of your choosing, and a rare opportunity to secure for yourself that unique kind of satisfaction that can only come from one being able to do something useful for oneself by oneself.

What this manual means to you, is simple: except for the court fees associated with the filing, it will cost you next to nothing to legally change your name; and what is more, you will not need to contend with the lawyer's "mysterious mumbo-jumbo" (not to speak of his high cost!) in undertaking one.

Though little known among many Americans, the fact of the matter is that, quite apart from the right of one to adopt a name of one's own choosing, by and large any individual (with a minimum knowledge of the basic procedures for doing it, of course!) has the civil, even the legal right, to file and process the application himself in court without having to employ the services of a lawyer.

What is true really, is that, except in very few instances - that is, in those uncommon cases involving the withholding of the necessary parental consent for a minor, or where there is a finding that the proposed name for an adult is bizarre or improperly motivated — there is really no serious need for the services of a lawyer in terms of the level of legal or technical complexity involved in the procedure.

---

*Quoted from an article titled, "Name Changes: A Rare Situation Where Law is Easier than You Might Think", part of a collective in The People's Law Review edited by Ralph Warner (Nolo Press), page 69.

MANUAL'S NATIONAL SCOPE

New York State's name changing procedures are employed in the manual for specific and detailed treatment of the procedures for deliberate reasons, and not by accident. New York is the acknowledged premier state in the nation in the development of decisional and statutory law in name changing, and its procedures on the subject have been widely copied and followed across the country. Hence, a prime objective in using New York as the focal point for detailed exposition here, is to use the state's practices as a proxy by which to illustrate the procedures of general use in most states of the nation. It is a task made easier and more practicable by one comforting fact which is of particularly special interest to the do-it-yourselfer: that, for the most part, the basic laws, rules and principles which underlie legal name changing are essentially identical from state to state across America, as are elements of the illustrated forms and procedures particular to New York.

Additionally, to further ensure that this book will be as universally useful and applicable as possible in each of the 50 states in the nation, we have taken pains to provide, in Chapter 6 (pp.61-65), a step-by-step procedure applicable for general filing in any state whatsoever, and in Appendix B (pp. 67-80), we further provide the basic name changing rules and basic information specific to each individual state.

The Publisher's continuing Gratitude to you, Our Readers.
Finally, we thank and urge this of you, our readers: Please continue to send us all those personal comments, opinions, thought or suggestions, you might have regarding this book; or news items, newspaper accounts or clipping of happenings from across the country you might come across. As always, just drop us a few lines at our address below (we prefer written communications, please). For us, you, the readers, are the **KING** or **QUEEN**, as the case may be! We very much value and welcome your feedback - always!!

Thank you again.

Newark, N.J.

DO-IT-YOURSELF LEGAL PUBLISHERS
60 Park Place
Newark, NJ 07102

CHAPTER  1

SOME PRELIMINARY BACKGROUND INFORMATION COMMON IN NAME CHANGE SITUATIONSS

A. Some Common Reasons Why People Change Their Names

There are a variety of motives and reasons which prompt individuals to want to change their names, and a variety of purposes and objectives they wish to accomplish by doing so. Among the most frequently cited motives, reasons or purposes, are the following:

1. The Sound or Pronunciation of Name:

One may have difficulty with, or dislike for, the way his present name sounds, or for the meaning, pronunciation, or spelling of the name. For example, an immigrant who originally came into the United States from a foreign country (or his parent or grandparent, before him), may have inherited an "ethnic" or "foreign" sounding name which may not be totally to his liking or convenience under the American environment. He may wish, perhaps, to have a more "American" sounding, probably shorter or easier-to-pronounce name, which would presumably de-emphasize his foreign connections.

2. Return to an Old Family Name:

Alternatively, persons may seek a change of name because they wish to return to a previously changed old family or ancestral name. The old name may probably denote for them much emotional or psychological meaning rooted in the family history. One's immigrant ancestors,, for example (say one's parents or grandparents), may have previously changed the family name to an "American" name upon first coming to the United States, but for one reason or another (e.g. the desire to return to your historical roots to maintain a sense of continuity), you, yourself, may happen to take a liking to or preference for that original ancestral name, choosing to return to it, instead.

3. For Sociological or Historical Reasons:

Many persons, predominantly of black American extraction, often change their birth names for the reason that they honestly consider them to be or to symbolize a "slave name" – that is, one derived from or taken after the name of whites (or even literally forced upon them in slavery era) and having no connection with their true African ancestry, heritage, or origins. Many famous blacks off-handedly come to mind who have changed their names ostensibly on such grounds: Kareem Abdul-Jabbar (from Lew Alcindor); Malcolm X (from Malcolm Little), and Muhammad Ali (from Cassius Clay), to name just a few.

4. Return to a Woman's Maiden Name:

A married woman who, upon marriage, had assumed her husband's name as is often customary, may at one point in time become concerned about losing her own family name forever, and may want to recapture and preserve that maiden name by reverting back to her maiden name. Or, a woman who has been divorced from her former husband may simply want to stop using the ex-husband's surname and assume either her maiden name, or a new one altogether, as a way of putting that not-particularly-pleasant episode of her past farther behind her.

5. Sheer Dislike of Present Name:

For one reason or the other peculiar to you or your peculiar circumstances, you may simply have a dislike for the name you were given at birth (or upon marriage), or feel it unfitting to your outlook or unrepresenting of the "real you". (A man, for example, who grew up only to find that he is of homosexual persuasion, for example, may wonder what in the world he is doing with a "macho" name like **JOHN WAYNE**!)

6. Change to a caring Stepfather's Name:

Often-times, a divorced woman having the custody of a child from her previous marriage, or the mother of a child born out of wedlock, may find herself saddled alone with the job of raising the child. The child's father may have abandoned the child providing no financial or emotional support or even having any contract with or interest in the child even from his infancy. The mother, under such circumstances, may want to change the child's last name out of the premise that changing the name more accurately reflects the reality of the father's apparent rejection of the child. This frequently happens most especially in situations where a divorcee mother remarries and then begets other children from her new marriage, and may thus want the child (or children) from the first marriage to bear the second husband's surname, which would also be the same name as those borne by the child's half-siblings from the second marriage. Undertaking the change of a child's name to take after the stepfather, is also thought of in such context as a special demonstration of appreciation on the part of the children from the previous marriage for their stepfather's care for them, and a solid step in the direction of forging a sense of common identity, closeness and togetherness by all as a family.

7. Change of Minor's Name to a Caring Guardian's:

A person who has been a guardian of another person's child, may want the child to have his (the guardian's) name as a mark of love, common identity or closeness between them. Or, as it also happens quite often, the ward (the object of the guardianship) himself may be the one who desires and asks for such a change to the name of the guardian.

8. Some Miscellaneous Reasons Relating to Changing the Minor's Name:

In so far as minor children are concerned, the circumstances under which the need for them to change their names arise may fall under the following:

--to correct spelling or typographical errors in the name on the original birth certificate.
--to legitimize a particular parentage or paternity brought about either because of a voluntary desire on the part of the parent(s) or by judicial decree of paternity.
--to conform the child's name when there has been a formal change of the family name (i.e., the surname) by the parents through court petition. *(As a rule applicable in most jurisdictions, when the parents legally change their family name, the surname of the minor children, if their names are clearly listed in the parent's court petition, will be deemed to be automatically changed as well to the parent's new Surname.)*

9. **To Take After the True Father's Name:**
In some instances, a person may have grown to adulthood with a family name (surname) derived from a man generally believed to be his father only to find out later that the supposed father was truly not his real father. (The supposed "father" may have been only a man who, though married to the mother at the time of the person's birth, did not father the child but had to be named after the child any way because the mother necessarily needed to "look good".)

10. **To Conform to a Professional Image or Lifestyle:**
Some may wish to change their names based largely on their lifestyles or their profession. For example, movie stars or aspirants, people in the media or the theater and the like, often prefer a more simple or catchy, non-ethnic name that may be easier to pronounce or to remember or recognize.

B. The two Basic Methods by Which Names are Changed

There are **two** basic methods by which one may change one's name: (I) change by common law method (commonly called the "common usage" method; and (ii) change by court order or proceedings (commonly called the "written law" or "legal" method).

1. The First Method: Change by Common Law Method or Common Usage

By a long-standing common law understanding held all across the United States, in practically every state in the nation a resident who desires to change his (her) name or to adopt one, may do so without ever making an application to any court or needing it's authorization. The rule is simple. At common law, absent improper or fraudulent motive, a person may adopt any name by which he chooses to be known, even without using any statutory procedure. *To put it simply, what this means is this: you may simply pick a name you want to answer or change to, and then proceed to use that chosen name over and over again on a consistent and prolonged basis and that chosen name will be just as legal and valid for you to assume, providing the reason behind the change is in no way for illegal, criminal or fraudulent purposes and/or is not occasioned by an intent to avoid a legitimate obligation or to interfere with the rights of others.*

A name changed or assumed by the common law method is, for all intents and purposes, the person's legal name rightfully assumed in all respects—just as legitimate and valid as one changed by a court order. In deed, in New York State, as in most states in the United States, the courts have held that the judicial or court method of changing ones name is merely an "affirmance and aid of the common law" method of accomplishing the same thing. A 1996 decision in New Jersey by that State's Courts, sums up the common law rule fairly well this way:

> "There is nothing in the common law prohibiting a man from taking another name if he so desires, nor is there any penalty or punishment for so doing, except that if a man assumes another name with the purpose of thereby defrauding another, he might, perhaps, be enjoined from the use of such name. The Statue(s) [of most states on this question]...do(es) not repeal the common law by implication or otherwise, but merely gives an additional method of effecting a change of name, one whereby a record may be kept of change of name..."*

---

*in re:Witsenhousen, 42 N.J.L.J.183(1919)

In a word, the common law rule is that the court method is merely a formalized method of confirming or acknowledging a name which could just as simply have been assumed or changed by merely using that name on a repeated and prolonged basis, and that a change by court proceedings is no more or less legal than a change by common usage!

2. The Second Method: Change By Court Order

While, admittedly, a change of name could more simply be effectuated by the mere act of adopting a preferred name with no court authorization, nevertheless a provision is made in every state for a more formal way of changing one's name—that is, change through court proceedings and a court order.

When the change is sought in this manner, the procedure by which it is effectuated is more or less spelled out by statute (i.e., a written law). Each state has its own specific laws and procedures which govern the court-oriented name change within the given state. In general, however, the rules and procedures are basically identical from state to state in the broad principles which underlie the process.

Stated in general terms, the court-oriented procedure involves essentially the following elements for virtually every state: the submission ("filing") of a written petition (also called by names like "certificate" or "application") to the appropriate local court, and the consideration and approval of the petition by a formal order of the court signed by the judge thereby authorizing the person to answer the proposed name. Depending on the requirement of the particular state involved, a hearing may often have to be held before the court may approve the petition, with an opportunity afforded any interested persons who interpose objection to the proposed name change to appear and be heard, and a public notice of the proposed change may further have to be given in some form, often by publication in a local newspaper, and so forth.

[For a further but more elaborate examination of the exact procedures involved in judicially changing a name, please see the chapters ahead, especially Chapters 4 through 6.]

C. Some Practical Advantages of the Court Order Method of Changing Name

Sure enough, it is true that changing one's name simply by common usage is at least as valid and lawful as changing it by judicial proceedings, and that, furthermore, the common usage method of changing a name will also cost you nothing while requiring you to expend **no** time, money or energy to seek the approval of a court. And, true enough, the common usage method is one that is not limited to a particular category of people or states, and can just as easily be employed by virtually everyone all across the United States to adopt a given name.

In spite of all these, the fact is that many people, in deed most, who seek to change their names still choose to do so through the court proceedings avenue.

The big, curious question, obviously, is why? Why this apparent paradox? Why would so many still take to the courts given the apparent relative simplicity and inexpensiveness of accomplishing the same end through the common usage method? The reason this is so can simply be summarized in one phrase: some distinct practical advantages which, in the real world, the court method enjoys over the common usage method of changing one's name.

The principal advantages of changing a name the judicial way, include the following: **1.** The procedure is relatively speedy and definite; it provides a public record by which the change of name is definitely and specifically established; and name change done by this method is more provable even after the person doing the change or the witnesses thereof are long dead. Since many relevant records and documents (such as the court order which authorized the change of name, birth certificates, sworn statements, record of hearings, where applicable, and the like) are filed with the court at the time of the judicial name change, it is thereby far easier to verify or to establish the change than would a change of one's name by merely assuming a certain name and being called by it, especially in a distant future when all the contemporaneous witnesses may have either died or moved away.

2. A second category if advantages possessed by the judicial method, has to do with the apparent inherent bias held by the public and civil institutions in favor of the name changed through the court. To put it simply, you can say all you wish in praise of the supposed virtues of changing a name by the "common usage" route—its lack of expense, relative lack of accountability to any court, absence of bureaucratic formalities, etc. *But after all is said and done, the simple fact of the matter is that the average person will sooner discover one profound reality, namely, that it frequently takes him or her far less time and hassles to get the court's approval to his (her) name change application than it would take him trying for the rest of his life to convince the public and the bureaucracies that the name he assumed through "common usage" is just as legal or valid.* A well established reality is that, as a practical matter, various agencies, government bodies, businesses, organizations, financial institutions, and the public at large, will be reluctant to accept a name changed or assumed by common usage, frequently viewing it, instead, with skepticism and suspicion. Frequently, the authorities will not just take your word for it— that is, without a showing of some kind of "official documentation", which, in many peoples minds, usually means a court order!

In deed, the case has been legitimately made by people well experienced in such matters, that by and large most people, especially the establishment personnel of society (in the governments, courts, financial institutions, business and the like), are probably not even aware that a "common usage" change is just as lawful and valid a way of changing one's name, and that such persons routinely believe only that which they can see "in writing" on paper signed by a judge. *In sum, the point, simply, is that as a practical matter, an "official" name change document from a court generally commands the* **unquestioned** *acceptance of your new name by everyone, while a name changed simply by common usage would often generate precisely the opposite experience for you.*

3. **Thirdly, a kind of "advantage" enjoyed by the judicial method of adopting a name,** is that one is able to say, categorically, that the method is accepted as legal and valid universally in all states across the board, with no exception. Strictly speaking, such claim cannot be made for a name changed by common usage. While it is true that in the overwhelming majority of States change made by common usage is, at least in theory,

considered lawful side by side with the judicially changed name, nevertheless, **experts**[*] have, upon a close scrutiny, been able to spot some handful of states where the validity of the common usage method itself is in question.

It is pointed out, for example, that in some states the enacted laws governing change by judicial method are worded in such a way as to imply that the **only** way to change one's name is by doing it the judicial way. The point here, then, is that this element of ambiguity contained in the laws of admittedly a handful of states on the subject may make the legality of change of name by "common usage" a not-so-certain one, at least in some states under certain circumstances—a handicap not at all possessed by making a change through the judicial avenue.

4. **Finally, there is this "advantage" of some sort possessed by the judicial method.** For the rather obvious reason that minors cannot ordinarily make major decisions solely on their own, change of name by the common usage route is generally not available to minors in virtually all jurisdictions. In most states, minors may not change their names (or, more correctly, have it changed for them by others) **except** by court order only.

NOTE: It is perhaps relevant for readers to note this in this connection. Classify it as an "advantage" or a "disadvantage", if you like. But, be aware that for all practical purposes, once you have changed your name by court method, you should just as well forget about ever having to change your name by any other method; generally, you will most likely be unable to adopt any other name (even to change back to your old name) thereafter—unless you again do so through the same formal procedure of a court of law!

D. Some Mistaken Notions Concerning Name Change: What a Change of Name Does Not Do For You.

There are a few mistaken beliefs and impressions common among the general public as to the true meaning or effect of changing one's name. Prominent among these notions are the following:

1. Many people often get the idea that by legally (judicially) changing one's name to the family name borne by a particular person, say a stepfather's, it necessarily establishes, by that fact alone, the existence of a legal father-child relationship between such two parties. Not at all.

The Situation more frequently arises in a stepfather-stepchild situation—where a child who was born of a different father or an earlier marriage follows the mother, upon her remarriage to another man, into the new household. The new husband of the mother may decide to change the stepchild's name to the new husband's (now the child's new stepfather) in the belief that such a move alone is in and of itself tantamount to legally changing the stepfather-stepchild relationship to a father-child one.

---

[*] See Edward J. Bander's "Change of Name and Law of Names", at p.5. Bander cites these examples: The State of Pennsylvania's Statute (written law) on the subject specifically states that it is unlawful to assume a different name except by court proceedings; Oklahoma's statute indicates that the statutory method is exclusive, that no change of name will be permitted except as provided by the statute, or by marriage, decree of divorce or adoption.

In truth, however, legally changing a name does not do any such thing. A legal change of name is **only** that—all it changes is only the name of the applicant, and little else. It certainly does not change the objective legal parentage of the person whose name is changed, be it in fact or in the eyes of the law.

2. Similarly, it is often thought by some that the fact that one's child has changed his or her surname to a different name directly alters the parent's parental legal responsibility towards that child, and, in effect, necessarily relieves one of continued responsibility to support or care for that child; or relieves the child of his/her duty to remain under the parent's custody or control. Not at all. In point of fact, all rights, duties and responsibilities which would normally exist between a parent and the child—obligation of support or care, right of visitation and contact, inheritance or custody rights, etc—remain intact, totally unaffected and unaltered one way or the other by the mere fact that a child legally changed his (her) name.

3. A legal name change of a minor (or, for that matter, an adult) is not the same thing as legally **adopting** the minor, and one is not a substitute for or the equivalence of the other [See "Achieving Name Change Through Adoption Proceedings," p. 22]

4. The mere fact of being married does not, in and of itself, necessarily change a woman's last name to that of her husband. For that to happen, the woman must, herself, take some definite affirmative steps—she must proceed to actively and commonly answer and use as her's that last name of the husband.

5. As might be imagined, legally changing one's name does not transform your innate character or identity in the sense of making you a "different person" other than who you are—you are still the same man or woman that you are, who was born at the same locality, on the same birth date, by the same parents, with the same history, background, attributes or record, and so forth, at least in the eyes of the law.

6. Legally changing you name does not rid you of any otherwise legitimate obligation you might have had to your family or to society—it does not, for example, wipe out your debts or make them inapplicable to you. They still exist, and they remain **yours** in the eyes of the law.

E. The Two Basic Categories of Name Change Applicants

Basically speaking, there are two broad categories by which applicants are classified, and which make some difference in the procedures followed in handling a given application for a name change. They are: (1) the adult's category, and (2) the minor's category.

1. Adults:

By and large the courts would and do approve an application for a name change that is made by a person of an "adult" age on his or her own behalf. Only if, in the court's view, the purpose or effect of the proposed name change is to defraud others or to evade a legitimate obligation or unduly infringe on the rights of others, would the courts generally deny such applications. (Under New York's rule, and most other states', an adult is one who is 18 years of age or over.)

2. Minors or Infants:

In applications involving minors (generally a person just 18 years of age or under), the rules governing the court's approval of such applications are somewhat more strict.

To begin with, a minor may not directly make the application himself (herself). An adult third party, usually one or both of the parents, or a guardian, must make the application for and on the minor's behalf, and must also grant their written consent for the minor to change his name. Secondly, before it would accept to accord its approval to a proposed change of name for a minor, the court would often require that there be what it considers a **"compelling" reason** for the proposed change. And if the court (i.e., the judge who is considering the application) should feel that there are no compelling reasons brought forth by the adult parents or guardian for wanting to change the minor's name, the application will probably be denied. The minor involved would then have to wait; his chance to take another crack at it (if, of course, he still desires), will come only by a reapplication by the minor himself when he attains the age of adulthood.

What kinds of circumstances are considered "compelling" in the court's eyes? In general, the purpose or reason for a proposed name change is deemed **"compelling"** when, in the court's opinion, the **"best interest"** of *the* minor child himself would be substantially served or enhanced by the proposed new name; or when, in the opinion of the court, *the minor himself* stands to gain substantial benefit by the change, an inheritance, for example, of a substantial asset, or a new feeling of well-being or of identity with a new family, or of being loved by a family. *It is, in other words, the minor's own "best interests" (as the court sees them) that are the relevant and paramount considerations herein, not what the parent(s) or guardian may independently want or prefer for the minor.*

F. Handling Objections to a Minor's Proposed Change of Name

As a general rule in almost every state, when an application is made for an infant's (i.e., a minor's) name to be changed, a natural parent or legal guardian is normally entitled to be given notice of such an application, and further has a standing legal right to file an objection to the proposed change of name—if the parent or guardian is opposed to it.*

---

*True, in the case of an adult petitioner, an objection may equally be raised—say by a spouse or by a child. However, objections in such situations are far less frequent or as heatedly contested.

In certain states, though, including New York, a person who is considered **"socially or civilly dead"** (a person incarcerated for life, for example), does not have this legal standing and is deemed to have forfeited the rights to raise such an objection.

Supposing some objections are raised, what happens then? Generally, when this arises, the court would usually set the matter down for a hearing at which time it will take testimony from all parties concerned. Depending on the nature of the evidence gathered therefrom, the court may either dismiss the objections and grant the petition, or it may accept the objections as having a valid basis and deny the request for the proposed change.

By and large, objections are more common in respect to petitions for minors. When confronted with a parent's objection to a proposed change in the name of the child, the courts, *in attempting to determine whether the change should be permitted even in spite of the objection, or be permitted without the consent of one of the parents, have generally employed the welfare of the child—the so-called "best interest of the child"—principle as the guiding and compelling considerations.* * In this connection, a well-grounded principle of law generally recognized by the courts is that the child's father who often is the objecting party, is said o have a **"protectable interest"** in having this child bear the parental surname in accordance with the usual custom, even in circumstances when the mother may have been awarded legal custody of the child. For this reason, where, in the court's evaluation, the motivation behind the proposed change of a minor's name is merely to save the mother and the child from minor inconvenience or embarrassment, the courts would not generally authorize such a change over the objection of a father.

**An objection raised under one or more of the following situations by a parent or guardian has generally little or no chance of being upheld by the court: ** **

(i) Where the minor child involved expressly wants the name change, and a sufficient case is made that the parent (usually the father) whose name the child now bears, has not shown much care, love or devotion for the child.

(ii) Where a good case is made that the objecting parent has not shown much interest in the minor. Example of that would be a showing that he has neglected to make payments for the minor's support or to visit with the minor for a considerable length of time.

---

* See, for example: Clinton v. Morrow, 220 Ark 337.247 SW 2d 1015; Mark v. Kahn, 333 Mass 517, 131 NE 2d 758,53 ALR 2d 908; Sobel v. Sobel, 46 NJ Super 284, 134 A2d 598; and Laks v. Laks (1975) 25 Ariz.App.58, 540 p.2d 1277

** For cases dealing with the issue of naming children at birth where the parents have different last names or disagree on the name to be given the child, and the mother has custody of the child, see Jacobs v. Jacobs, 309 N.W.2d 303 (Minn.1981) In re: Schiffman, 28 Cal. 3d 640, 169 Cal. Rptr. 918, 620 p.2d 579 (1980); In re: M.L.P., 621 S.W.2d (Tex. Civ. App. 1981; concerns dispute over first and middle names only); and Hurta v. Hurta, 25 Wash. App. 95, 605 p.2d 1278 (1979). In a 1984 New Jersey case, for example, the court ruled that, there is necessarily no presumption favoring the father's right to have his child retain his name, and concluded that the mother of a child, less than two years of age, was entitled to have her child's surname changed to her maiden name where the child had lived with the mother almost exclusively since his birth, was too young to have achieved any significant identification with his last name, and his father's interest in his welfare had been so modest as to be nonexistent. (Application of Rossell by Yacono, 196 N.J. Super.109, 481 A. 2d 602 (L. 1984).

(iii) Where it is shown that the objecting parent has engaged in conducts which bring shame, scorn, derision, or public notoriety to name which the minor child (or the spouse) seeks to change.

On the other hand, an objecting parent (usually the father) has a good chance of being upheld by the court under the following circumstances, if the objecting parent can show:

(i) That he has frequently visited with and contributed regularly to the support of the child; and/or

(ii) That he has generally manifested a sincere affection, devotion and good relationship with the child, and that the change of name is all too likely to upset that relationship; and/or

(iii) That he has not abandoned or deserted the child, or surrendered natural ties of parental interest and association with him; and/or

(iv) That he has conducted himself in a manner that generally gives credit to the present name which the infant bears.

G. It's Possible The Court May Deny Your Petition. What Might be the Grounds For This, and Your Remedy?

As a practical matter, the court to which a petition for name change is presented may, in actuality, refuse to grant the application. It is totally in the sole, al beit "reasonable", discretion of the court as to whether to grant a given petition, or to refuse to grant it.

Are there any limitations to the court's discretion, though? Definitely yes. The general rule is that the court may not abuse the wide discretion allowed it in his subject matter, and should it become apparent that the court's discretion has been abused in refusing to grant a given petition, or that the court acted in an arbitrary manner, then the court's decision is subject to review and correction on appeal to an appellate court.

What specific circumstances will be considered improper or unjustified for a court's refusal to grant a given petition for change of name? That's generally difficult to determine, much less to predict. Every case turns on its own facts, and frequently the facts of each case are somewhat different from those of one another. Nevertheless, as a general guideline, the rule is that some **special** and **"substantial reason"** must exist before the court may be justified in denying an application to change a name.

*Examples of special or substantial reasons would be something like: ***

- a choice with an unworthy motive, such as a demonstrable intent to change one's name for fraudulent purposes (such as for the purpose of doing something illegal or criminal, or in order to conceal one's identity to evade the law);

---

* See, for example, for some of the differing reasons, In re: Knight, 36 Colo. App.187, 537 p.2d 1085 (1975); application of M, 91 N.J. Super. 296, 219 A.2d 906 (Co. 1966)

- a choice likely to have an undesirable impact on others other than the applicant, or tending to "interfere with the rights of others" or having that actual effect (such as capitalizing or "cashing in" on the good name or reputation of some other person, or implicating another person in one's deeds);
- the choice of name that is bizarre or obscene, or unduly lengthy, ridiculous or offensive to common decency and good taste.
- The choice of name is likely to affect the interest of a wife or child of the applicant in an adverse way.
- a choice tending to defraud or mislead or misrepresent
- a choice of name is, for example, racist, obscene or otherwise likely to provoke violence, arouse passions, or inflame hatred. (Application of Dengler, 1979, 287 N.W. 2d 637, appeal dismissed 100 S.ct. 2913)

That which constitutes a good or substantial reason for the court to deny an application in a particular situation, however, may not usually coincide with a given petitioner's notion of that. The court, it should be noted, is not subject to the whims of every name change petitioner.   Thus, for example, it has been held by a Nebraskan court that a petition for a change of name by an adult husband and father was properly denied on the grounds that it would change the name of the petitioner's wife and their minor children. In that case, the court having especially been shown evidence that the applicant had previously changed his name several times over, accepted the objections of the applicant's wife to the proposed name change based upon her claims that the change will result in injuries to the feelings and sensibilities of the wife and children and bring harm to the standing in society which they had acquired under the applicant's name. Likewise, the refusal by the court of a married woman's petition to change her name to that of her deceased former husband for the sole purpose of prosecuting a wrongful death court action has been held to be proper by a Texas court.

In sum, the central point here is that there is no predicable pattern or fixed set of grounds for all cases. In any given instance, the court may look upon some reasons advanced for a proposed name change with sympathy, while looking upon some other reasons coldly. What may satisfy the courts of one state as a justifiable ground to approve an application may be totally unacceptable to the courts of another jurisdiction, in light of the fact, especially, that the detailed specifics of the relevant laws and decisions of the states differ from one another. Nevertheless, all these aside, it is equally valid for one to make this assertion: *by and large the courts adhere to the basic principle that, except for those rare instances where there are a finding of silly or insufficient reasons or of fraudulent or criminal purpose, the courts would loath or be reluctant to refuse an adult's application to assume another name.* *

** See, for example, a 1947 Pennsylvania case which held that though the court has a wide discretion in passing upon a petition for change of name, nevertheless a court in doing so will exercise its discretion in such a way as to comport with good public. (Petition of Falcucci, 50 A. 2d 200, 355 Pa 588, 1947)

In deed, there's abundant evidence (from several court decisions in many states) which plentifully suggest that *a substantial number among the judges who handle name change matters all across the nation may have already made a moral, pragmatic judgement in favor of the position that the courts should encourage, not discourage, the use by the public of the judicial channel to change their names, and that the courts should simply decide on the petitions in a generally liberal and favorable manner.* The judges strongly imply that, given the fact that the applicant who applies to the court for a proposed new name could just as easily have opted to assume and answer the name, anyway, under the "common usage" rule, and doesn't necessarily have to seek the court's permission to do so, the court system ought to reciprocate in kind to the public's courtesy by facilitating, not hindering, the process of changing one's name through the courts. In taking this position, Judges have often expressed the view that one distinctive reason why it is more desirable to encourage the public to change their names through the courts, rather than through common usage, is that doing so through the courts will at least make the assumed name a matter of public record far much easier to verify, if nothing else.*

---

* In a case, for example, involving a California petitioner whose application for name change was denied by the state's lower court for the reason that the petitioner had declared bankruptcy as a result of which his financial obligations to others had been discharged, the appellate court upheld the petitioner, on appeal, and granted his application to change his name. The appellate court noted in its ruling, that the petitioner could have changed his name anyway (by the "common usage" route) without seeking the court's authorization, and that granting the petitioner's application by the court would probably be of greater preference and benefit to his creditors in that it would at least make the name change a matter of public record. In another case, also decided in California, wherein a third party filed objections to a proposed change of name to a name which the petitioner had used for some 14 years, the court ruled that under the circumstances pertaining to the case, the proposed name "constituted petitioner's legal name, just as much as if he had borne it from birth," adding that the petitioner could just as well have answered the proposed name without resorting to the court, and that "the purpose of the petitioner in filing this proceeding was to establish a legal record of that which he had already legally done many years before." [See 8 Cal. (2)608, 67 p. (2)94, and 35 Cal. App. (2) 723, 96 p. (2) 958, for the above cited cases, respectively.]

CHAPTER  2

THE MARRIED PERSON AND CHANGE OF NAME: THE BASIC CURRENT LAW AND PRACTICES

What are the rights of a married woman with respect to the use of her maiden name, or the use of the surname of her husband? What legal problem may arise when a woman who is divorced wishes to resume her maiden name or the name of a prior husband? As for the married man, under what circumstances may he be permitted, or not be permitted, by the court to change his own names or the family name? What are the legal implications that may arise when either the husband or the wife changes his/her name during marriage? These are some of the more significant questions that have become increasingly relevant in the field of name change law in recent times.

A. The Woman's Case as the Classic Case:

In England from which the United States derives much of her legal principles and traditions, the old common law conception was to see the married woman as one and the same person as her husband, a mere extension of him. **As *Blackstone, the famous common law jurist,*** so well summed it up, "by marriage the husband and wife are one person in law; that is, the very being or legal existence of the woman is suspended during the marriage, or at least is incorporated and consolidated into that of the husband, under whose wing, protection, and cover, she performs everything;...For this reason, a man cannot grant anything to his wife, or enter into covenant with her for the grant would be to suppose her separate identity, and to covenant with himself."*

However, over the period of many centuries, the status of the married woman has undergone tremendous changes so that, under the so-called Married Women's Acts of the recent times, the married woman has been largely "emancipated" from much of such legal disabilities of the past. Today, almost everywhere the married woman is now considered a separate and distinct legal entity from her husband, with the full right to separately enter into all types of contracts or economic relationships with anyone.

B. The Main Situations Under Which Married Woman Seek to Change Their Names

1. Change from Woman's Married Name to a Name Other than Her Husband's:

To be sure, it doesn't happen too often. Nevertheless, it does happen sometimes. A married woman, perhaps in the midst of some matrimonial difficulties, may seek to change her surname from that of her husband, to that of, say, her first husband's.

---

* Commentaries, 442., as quoted in "Change of Name and Law of Names" by Edward J. Bander (1973)

Admittedly, as is probably to be expected, the courts have differed in their approaches on this issue. **In one Missouri case**, for example, * a married woman's application to have her surname changed to a name different from her husband's was ruled permissible where no evidence existed that the change will result in harm to her husband, future children or creditors, and the new name was found not to be bizarre or obscene or offensive. But in **another case in South Carolina,** one of the earlier cases of this variety ever to come up in the United States, a wife's petition to be allowed to change her name from that of her husband to that of her first husband was denied by the court as being "wrong in principle."

By and large, however, the more common attitude which predominates among the nation's courts on this issue seems to be one of reluctance to grant a married woman authorization to assume the name of someone other than the husband—**except** where it is done with the consent of the woman's present husband.**

As a general proposition, an application which possesses more of the following elements has the best chance of being looked at favorably by the courts: evidence that the proposed name change will neither have disruptive effect on the family nor be harmful to the woman's husband's future children, or creditors; that the proposed name is not bizarre, obscene, or offensive; agreement among the woman and her husband and the children regarding the name to be answered by the children; the husband's affirmative support or consent; lack of reason to believe that the petition was filed for illegal, fraudulent or immoral purposes; and a showing that the wife otherwise meets all the statutory requirements for changing a name as prescribed under the law.

2. Change from a Woman's Name to the Husband's name Upon Marriage:

With the exception of just a few jurisdictions in the nation, by and large there are no legal provisions expressly requiring a married woman to adopt her husband's surname upon marriage. Quite to the contrary, actually the rule is that the married woman who so prefers may, by and large, retain and continue to use her maiden name upon marriage— providing she uses it exclusively, consistently and nonfraudulently.*** However, while it is true that even under the old common law rule the woman was never under any legal compulsion to adopt her husband's name, it should nevertheless be noted that it has been, and still remains to this day, a very strong and widely accepted custom with deep roots into the past for the wife to do exactly that—to go ahead anyway and adopt the husband's surname upon marriage. The common rule of law here is that, though the woman is not

---

*   (MO App.) 527 SW 2d 402

**   See, for example, the following rulings by the courts: Strikwerda, 216 Va 470, 220 SE 2d 245; Application of Lawrence (1975) 133 NJ Super 408, 337 A.2d 49.

***The Rights of Women, p.245. See, also, for example, this case cited in that report; Krupa vs. Green, 114 Ohio App. 497 112 N.E. 2d 616 (1961)

required by law to answer her husband's name upon marriage, nevertheless if she were to commit herself to the husband's surname by answering and using it, then she, at that point, has in effect accepted it as her name for all legal intents and purposes.

Recent research * on this issue, found in 1973 only one state, Hawaii, and Puerto Rico, had a law which clearly and unambiguously stated that the wife and children must use the husband's name, and not even a single case could be turned up where a judge ordered a woman to use her husband's name for all purposes. A few cases (just five or six of them) were found in a few states, however, where a married woman who refused to use her husband's surname or to re-register under her husband's name upon marriage for, say, a driver's license or to vote, was actually penalized by a court—mostly by way of being denied some other rights, such as the right to vote, or the right to have the woman's driver's license issued in her maiden name, or to have the naturalization papers issued in her maiden name. But, even then, the study reported that "the number of reported penalties is so low, in part, because most of the laws are ambiguous...In fact, the chances are slim that she (a married woman who does not use her husband's surname) will be actually penalized by the courts or will lose any of the legal rights mentioned...however, the chances of her encountering resistance by banks, department stores, and employers run high."**

Is there any possible cure-all for this problem for the average woman?
Yes, there is. Fortunately, there is available to the woman one truly sure way by which the married woman can pretty much put this issue to rest for good and ensure once and for all that she'll not encounter resistance, harassment or penalties from state officials or the society with respect to not using the husband's name. The remedy is simply for the woman to change her name formally through the court procedure.

In all states – whether in those which by laws or court decisions require that the woman's name change automatically upon marriage as a matter of law,*** or in those which allow the woman the option to choose to use or not to use the husband's name on the understanding that it is only be custom and not by law that the woman assumes the husband's surname – the use of formal court procedure to assume a desired name will be just as effective in protecting the married woman against any kind of harassment or the imposition of penalties for preferring a given name. As one report sums it up, "Once a woman obtains a legal document setting forth her legal surname, state officials cannot penalize her for refusing to use her husband's name...Women report that a legal document also works like magic in eliminating the objections of banks, department stores, and employer personnel."****

---

* See The Rights of Women (Bantam Books: 1984), p..245
** The Rights of Women, pp. 245 & 247
*** Such states are designated as the following: Alabama, Connecticut, Illinois, Iowa, Kentucky, Maine, Oregon, and Vermont. (The Rights of Women, Appendix C.)
**** The Rights of Women, p. 247

3. Change from Married to Maiden Name, after Divorce:

For many women, the one time in their lives they may have to give some serious thoughts to the idea of changing their names is when a divorce occurs. If, on the one hand, a woman should decide that she prefers to keep on using her married name (i.e., the divorced husband's surname) after being divorced, it is perfectly within her rights to do so under the prevailing laws and procedures of the vast majority of states today—providing she remains exclusive and consistent in the use of the name, and that she in no way deceptively passes herself off to the public as still married to the ex-husband.

If, on the other hand, a woman should decide that she prefers to change back to her maiden name (or to a prior name) after a divorce, she is equally permitted under the law of the vast majority of states to do so. In deed, in this connection, the laws of most states now require the courts to grant resumption of the woman's maiden or pre-nuptial name upon divorce as a routine matter—if the woman so requests. Hence, in most states, the woman's change of name upon divorce is virtually routine and automatic, built into the divorce procedure itself as an integral part of the process. Some courts* have, in fact, gone even further to hold that even where, for one reason or the other, the woman either fails to request it or is unable to change her name at the time of her divorce proceedings, that's not a waiver or forfeiture of her right subsequently to seek to do so judicially and that she can always undertake that at any later date she chooses.

---

* See Ogle v. Circuit Court, 10th (Now 6th) Judicial Circuit (S.D.) NW 2d 621. As of the time of the last count (1984), only a handful of states were listed as those still not having a law expressly allowing a divorced woman to resume her maiden (or prior) name. They are: Co., Fl., Id., Ky., La., Md., Miss., Mt., Neb., NM., ND., TN., UT., and Wy.

THE NEW YORK TIMES, ,JUNE 28, 1983.

Changing Women's Names

By SHARON JOHNSON

A New York City woman who is divorced and who earns more than $30,000 a year was recently rejected by a department store when she applied for credit under her maiden name. The store said it was sorry but it could not issue a credit card because it had no indication whether she paid her bills.

A struggling Los Angeles artist married an investment banker in 1970. The woman, who assumed her husband's surname, achieved considerable success. Now the couple are separated and the man is threatening legal action if his estranged wife continues to use his name in her work. She does not want to use her maiden name because she fears that buyers of paintings will not recognize it and her sales will decline.

These women are among the thousands of American women who have found that changing their names when they marry may affect their credit ratings, professional lives and personal identities.

Few Legal Restrictions

"Any woman who gets married today should think twice about changing her name," said Raoul Lionel Felder, a prominent Manhattan matrimonial lawyer. "It can have some serious repercussions, especially for women over 30 who have achieved some professional success. By taking her husband's name, a woman may lose a good credit rating, recognition for her achievements and contacts in her field."

Women face few legal restrictions in the use of names. Many states once required a woman to take her husband's surname upon marriage; in 1976 Hawaii became the last state to rescind such a provision. Now women, like men, may call themselves anything they choose as long as the name is not used for fraudulent purposes. Married women may retain their birth names, take their spouses' surnames, adopt hyphenated versions of both names or assume pen or other professional names.

Four states — Georgia, Hawaii, Iowa and Minnesota — require women and men to state on their marriage licenses what names they plan to use after the ceremony. The other states leave the matter open so that names can be changed at any time.

"Changing a name is easy," said

Marlene Zigmond, assistant director of the Center for a Woman's Own Name, a not-for-profit organization that seeks to end discrimination against women who wish to determine their names. "Sometimes, however, women encounter opposition from public officials, creditors and their own families."

For residents of New York State to change their name they need only notify the Social Security Administration, the Department of Motor Vehicles, the Board of Elections and professional licensing agencies, asking them to change their records and issue new forms of identification. Creditors, schools, employers and

---

Professional contact, credit and the recognition of achievements can be affected.

---

professional associations should also be informed.

There are no specific statutes governing name changes in New York and most other states. In some states court proceedings are necessary to change a name after divorce. For example, Indiana law provides that "if a woman requests restoration of her maiden or previous married name, the court shall grant such name change upon dissolution" of a marriage.

As for name changes in general, Gary Walker of the New York City Department of Consumer Affairs commented: "Creditors are the biggest problem. We get complaints from women who say that stores, banks and others won't extend them credit under their new names because they have no record of whether the women have paid their bills."

To avoid such problems he advises

women who assume their husbands' names to request creditors to incorporate their credit histories as unmarried women and any records of joint accounts. That way, he says, the history of the wife's credit rating will be preserved.

It also is wise for married women to be listed by their first names and birth names on credit cards so that they won't lose their identity on financial records. A woman who is listed as Mrs. John Smith rather than Mary Fisher Smith might have difficulty obtaining credit in the event of divorce or separation or if she changes her name while still married; creditors may assume that she has made no contribution to family finances or was not responsible for paying bills she incurred.

A woman who changes her name and is denied credit should ask for a written explanation of the denial. Then she or her lawyer should write a letter correcting any misinformation or pointing out circumstances of which the creditor may be unaware. The divorced New York City woman, for example, informed the department stores that she had worked throughout her marriage; only her husband's employer was listed in their records. The store issued her a credit card.

Keeping What They Have

Many female artists, journalists and professors and other professionals avoid changing their names when they marry because they have established their reputations under their names and do not want to start over under new ones. Some women, like the recently separated Los Angeles artist, face the opposite problem: They want to continue using their married names despite objections from their husbands or former husbands.

"Men cannot stop their wives or ex-wives from using the husband's name," said Mr. Felder, who has found that 15 percent of his clients resume their maiden names at the time of divorce. "As long as the woman isn't using his name to run up bills that he is not required to pay, she can continue to call herself Mrs. John Smith or whatever."

AUTHOR'S NOTE: Lest our readers be unduly misinformed, there are seemingly one or two rather serious misstatements in this article that seem worthy of note. We have in mind, first, the assertion in the article that "for residents of New York State to change their name they need only notify the Social Security Administration, the Department of Motor Vehicles...asking them to change their records and issue new forms of identification..." (Simply see, for example, Chap. 1, pp. 3-6, and STEP 8 of Chap. 4, pp.33, of the manual for some relevant realities which negate this assertion.)

And another assertion is obviously erroneous, namely, that: "There are no specific statues governing name changes in New York and most other states." (Simply see, for example, Appendix B of the manual, at pp. 67-80)

CHAPTER 3

SOME GENERAL RULES AND PROCEDURES
COMMON TO NAME CHANGE PETITIONS EVERYWHERE

A. Closeness of the Rules and Procedures Among Most States

In Appendix B, pp 67-80, you will find outlined a summary of the basic laws, rules and other state-specific information of relevance for undertaking judicial change of a personal name for **each** of the 50 states. In this present chapter, we shall address the more **general** rules and procedures broadly applicable in judicial name change in most of the United States. As already noted in an earlier chapter (see Chap. I. Section B(2) at p.4), *though it is true that each state has its own specific laws and procedures governing judicial name change within the given state, nevertheless, the real good news about this subject matter actually has to do with how vastly similar the procedures often are across the different states, not how different.* Of course, as it is probably to be expected in a subject such as this, some differences abound in the particulars and specific details of the procedures from one state to the other; but the procedures, as you will shortly discover in the succeeding pages, nevertheless remain broadly identical in the principles and purposes that underlie them. Notice such close similarities as you read along in the succeeding pages, as well as in Appendix B (pp. 67-80) thereof.

B. Where the Application is Made

For each state, the particular court (or, in certain states, the government agency or official) to which the application is presented, is specified by the state's written law (the "Statute"). These go by different names in different states – "civil court," "probate court," "surrogate court," the "superior" court, the "chancery" court, etc. – depending on the given state's designation. As a general rule, you will usually have to file for a name change in that branch of the proper court which is located in your county or district of **residence**, or of the minor's, if applicable.

C. General Nature of the Application

In general, you will have to commence your name change application by submitting ("filing") some sort of a written application – variously called also by such names as a "petition" or "certificate" - to the appropriate court in your locality. The specific contents of such application may differ from state to state. However, generally the major requirements could fairly be summarized as follows: specification of the grounds (reasons and purposes) for which the change is sought; the petitioner's name, residence address, date and place of birth; the proposed name; statement as to whether the applicant has been convicted of a crime* or adjudicated a bankrupt by a court of law, and if so, the details of same; statements as to whether there are any judgments or liens of record against him or her, and whether there are any legal actions or proceedings pending to which he or she is a party; statement concerning the petitioner's liability on any substantial commercial paper or bond or other major debts or obligations, if any; statement of the marital status of the petitioner and the names and ages of the minor children, if any, and the current nationality of the petitioner.

The petition must then provide for being properly signed, and then being "verified" (i.e., formally notarized or otherwise acknowledged) before it may be submitted to court.

[The sample forms supplied by the Do-It-Yourself Legal Publishers, as listed in Chapter 6 and Appendix A (pp. 1 & 66) of the manual, fairly well incorporates the essential information meeting most states' needs]

D. Publication Requirements

Depending on the state in which you live and file (see Appendix B, pp. 67-80, to determine this), you may be required to publish for a stated period of time some information or notice in a newspaper concerning the change of name. Often, what you are required to publish is one or more of the documents you submitted in the filing of your petition – the petition for the change itself (or a specific part of it), or the final order of the court granting the change, or a notice of name change or of the hearing on the petition, or a combination of these. In some states (e.g. New York), it is the judge that designates the particular newspaper in which the notice of name change is to be published, while in other states (e.g. California), the petitioner himself is allowed to select the paper.

Under the procedures of many states (e.g. Arizona and Utah), whether or not publication is to be undertaken in each individual case is optional – left to the discretion of the judge; he decides on a case-by-case basis and directs each petitioner as to whether to publish or not to. However, for the vast majority of states, where publication is at all applicable under the state's procedures, it's non-optional – all applicants are required to carry out a publication.

E. Times When Formal Notice to Parent or Guardian is Required.

The issue of giving a formal written notice of a hearing, or notice of the making of a petition for change of name, more commonly arises in situations where the subject of the proposed change of name is a minor. Statutes often stipulate that where the person whose name is sought to be changed is a minor, both **parents** (or the guardian), if alive, must preferably join in the petition. However, where there is only a single parent (or just a guardian) in the minor child's life, or where one of the two parents refuses to give his or her voluntary consent to the

---

* **Note**: Readers should note that while certain states require that the petitioner specify whether he has been convicted of a crime and give details thereof, the relevant statutes therein do not generally state that a conviction will bar an individual from obtaining a name change; they only require the petitioner to **state** whether or not he has been convicted—that is, to make full and honest disclosure. Thus, an ex-convict seeking a change of name will have to satisfy the court (as would anybody else) that the reason for the change is not for purposes of deceiving or defrauding anyone, and once done, he can be reasonably assured of the court's approval, ex-convict or not!

proposed change of the minor's name, it is customary for the law to require that the parent seeking the change should nevertheless give proper notice to the other (the non-consenting) parent, adequately informing him or her of the proposed change of the minor's name and the facts thereof. (The underlying premise for requiring this notification to the non-consenting parent, is that, with such bit of information, the non-consenting parent who is truly opposed to the proposal shall at least have been accorded the opportunity to file an objection and make his case with the court to prevent it, if so inclined!)

F. Residence Requirements
The general rule is that a person applying for a change of name must be a resident of the state or county where the application is made. The length of such residence differs from state to state, however (See Appendix B for details specific to individual states).

G. Consent Requirements Concerning Minors
Except for a few states where the age limit is twenty-one (21), in most states in the nation a minor (also called an "infant") is defined as a person eighteen (18) years of age or under. As has been mentioned in an earlier Section of this chapter (See Section E above), the one feature which generally distinguishes the name change petition for a minor from that of an adult, lies in the fact that in the minor's case his petition must usually be signed or otherwise consented to for him by a third party adult person or persons—the parent(s), guardian or custodian of the minor-- before it could be approvable by a court. Furthermore, as is the case with the state of New York's procedures, the statutes generally require the minor child himself to also "join" in the petition if he/she is over certain specified age, commonly 14 or 15, though still below the designated age of adulthood.

So important is the issue of parental consent in the eyes of the courts, that it is not uncommon for the courts to require it nonetheless even when the parents are separated or divorced. Only where it can be satisfactorily demonstrated to the court that a **"good cause"** or basis exists for which one or both parents are unable to join in or otherwise give their consent to the petition, will the courts probably be willing to waive that requirement and approve a minor's petition in spite of lack of parental support. A **"good cause"** would be, say, a showing of incompetence or of death by the other parent, or of his/her permanent absence from the home or country; or a de facto **"abandonment"** of the child by the parent as evidenced by failure on such parent's part to fulfil normal parental obligation of presence, love, care and support over a prolonged period of time.

[See Chapter pp. 7-10 and Sec. E above for more on consent issues generally]

H. Citizenship of Applicant and Changing of Name
Is being a United States citizen a prerequisite to the granting of a petition for a change of name? Must one be a citizen before one may apply or qualify? The answer seems to be, absolutely no. Aliens who are lawfully and properly admitted to the country are known to apply frequently to the courts in various states to have their names changed, and are known to win the courts' approval in about as large a number, the same as the citizens are treated. The conditions and requirements for securing the court's approval are more or less the same, except, perhaps,

that an Alien applicant would have to disclose his immigrant status in the petition, and would need to give notice of the changing of his name to the Immigration and Naturalization Service.

In deed, some court rulings relating to aliens have even suggested that since the alien has as much common law right as a citizen on the subject and could, anyway, change his name by "common usage" without the court's approval, it may be more desirable and prudent for the courts to make court-ordered name change relatively easy so as to at least make the changing of name by aliens a matter of public record for the greater benefit of society.*

An important avenue by which aliens change their names is to *do so as part of the naturalization proceeding leading from alien status to United States Citizenship.* Under a federal law, the (federal) courts have the power to grant, as well, the change of name of an alien applicant for naturalization, if so requested by the alien. In such a case, upon the (federal) judge making a decree approving the alien's naturalization into U.S. citizenship, the judge will issue the Certificate of Naturalization simply containing a clause therein to the affect that the former alien's pre-naturalization name has been change to a new, specified one.

I. Birth Certificates and Name Change

One question that often arises among those contemplating a judicial change of name, is: will my original birth certificate be physically corrected or changed in the appropriate government agency's records to reflect the new name?

The answer to this is varying. Under the rules of some states (say California's), it is required that upon the change of one's name a copy of the court's Order of Name Change be transmitted to the State's Bureau of Vital Statistics (if the person was born in the state) wherein the necessary correction would then be made in the applicant's birth certificate records. And under the rules of yet many other states (say, New York's), you may but you are not required to, give such formal notice of your name change to your state of birth's Bureau of Statistics, and only if you give such notification will the bureau make any corrections in the birth certificate or birth records as to the name change.

One point which often gets confused, however, needs to be clarified and clearly understood in this connection: namely, in most states, even when and if the state authorities enter information relating to the legal name change in the state's vital statistics records (or other records), this does not mean that the petitioner's **birth certificate** itself is physically changed, necessarily. It is important that the two issues be distinguished from each other, and not be confused. The point, simply, is that you could have your name changed in a court without necessarily having a new birth certificate issued to you. In fact, the more general rule across the country is that legally changing one's name does not directly entitle one to a new birth certificate. In a state like California or New York, for example, except in some limited special circumstances (e.g. in an adoption), the states' Bureaus of Vital Statistics will not issue a fresh revised birth certificate upon a person's birth certificate. All they'll usually do, upon the change being independently brought to their attention by the applicant by presentation of a certified copy of the court's Name Change Order, is to make an official notation on the original birth certificate indicating the changes made in the pre-existing name—but no new or fresh certificate reflecting just the new name will issue. (See Appendix C, "How to Get Birth & Death Records," at pp. 81-5 of the manual.)

---

* See 32 NYS (2) 264.

J. Name Change and "Sexual Orientation"

An issue that has become increasingly raised in recent times in connection with judicial change of name, has been what the attitude of the courts should be with respect to that group of petitioners with other than "mainstream" sexual orientation (e.g. transsexual and homosexuals)? The question is raised, for example: how should the petition of a male who proposes to change his name to a female's name for the reason of his sexual preference, be handled by the court?

As is to be predicted, the issue is one that has evoked varying answers, one that to this day remains as yet unresolved as a legal issue. There have at times been certain interesting, even unexpected, developments along the way, however. For Example, in a 1968 New York case,* a transsexual who has had his male organs removed and wished to have a female identity, was allowed a change of name from a male first name to a female first name. In granting the application, the presiding judge, **Judge Francis N. Pecora**, after entering into a most esoteric discussion of the erotic and sexual nuances involved in this field of human physiology, noted that "there is no chance that this petitioner will ever again function as a male either procreatively or sexually". The judge further made it categorically clear, however, that a fraud might be perpetrated on the public if this "female" could continue to masquerade as a member of the "male" brigade.

And in another case,** a homosexual graduate of a Law School who had been barred from openly "marrying" one of his sex, was reported to have legally changed his name from Jack Baker to Pat McConnell and then obtained a license to marry and actually married.

K. Achieving Name Change Through Adoption Proceedings

Aside from changing one's name through the filing of a petition for a name change in a local or state court of record, or doing so through a U.S. Federal District court as part of an alien's naturalization proceeding to become a United States citizen, there is a third important formal procedure by which an individual may judicially adopt another name: through a court adoption proceedings.*** True, the change of an adoptee's name is not a specific requirement for adoption under any state's rules and it is not necessary to have an adoptee's name changed in order to accomplish an adoption. Nevertheless, as a rather constant incidental in adoption proceedings, a change of name almost always accompanies the legal adoption of a child. In such a proceeding for an adoption, if the court approves the adoption application, the judge issues a decree of adoption which then provides, among other things, for a change of the adopted child's name as requested by the adoption application. Provision is also often made for the issuance of a new birth certificate in the child's new name.

---

*   In re: Anonymous, 293 N.Y.S. 834; 57 Misc. (2)813; Civil Court, New York County, Sept. 17, 1968.

**   Cited from Edward J. Bander's "Change of Name and Law of Names" at p.12, citing N.Y. Times, Jan. 7, 1973 p.55

*** Readers interested in the rules and procedures in respect to adoption proceeding may consult another volume published by the same publisher, "How to adopt a Child Without a Lawyer", authored by Benji O. Anosike.

CHAPTER 4

NEW YORK'S NAME CHANGE PROCEDURES: CHANGING THE NAME OF AN ADULT PERSON

A. New York State as the Representative Model for Most States.

As has been repeatedly emphasized in some earlier sections of this manual (see especially Chapter 3), though there are some differences alright in the **detailed particulars** of the procedures involved in judicially changing one's name, nevertheless the broad principles which govern these procedures are essentially similar from state to state. Generally, the procedures boil down to the filing of a petition (same as "application", "declaration" or "certificate") with the appropriate courts in which you set forth the new name to be taken and the reason for which you wish to change your name..

In this chapter (as well as in the next chapters that follow), we seek to detail some of those details and specifics which are necessarily state-specific to a single state, the state of New York. *The primary object in giving here an elaborate, detailed treatment of New York procedures is to employ this for illustrative purposes—as a "model" state whose procedures for judicially changing a name are amply demonstrative of the general procedures all across the United States.*

Employing New York for illustrative purposes, as is hereby intended, is a role which could not be more fitting for New York. For one thing, New York courts are reputed to be the pioneers in developing court decisional law in the area of name changing; the state happens to be one of the few which can legitimately boast of a long-standing, fully developed body of case laws, court decisions, and enacted statutes from which to draw as precedents. In matters concerning legal change of name, some states are quite detailed in the procedures to be followed, while others dispose of the subject in a sentence or two. New York, on its part, happens not only to have a statute which covers the matter at considerable length, but also has an extensive case laws and court rulings developed over a long period of time to go with it on a whole array of issues on the subject.

Even of still greater relevance for our purposes here, is this: the name changing requirements and procedures of New York State (as outlined below) are fairly representative of the general procedures followed in most States. All told, one truism can be fairly strongly asserted in this connection with all certainty: *if you are able to judicially change your name—or merely able to follow how to do so—in New York, you can equally change your name in just about every other state.* You would only need to use the same basic knowledge outlined in this and the next chapters (and your God-given common sense!) to get it all done.

B. Who May File a Petition and Where?

By and large, New York State's rules relating to changing a name by an adult (or even a minor) person follow a rather general principal that are equally common to most states. Under New York's rules, any adult resident of the state may make a formal, written application (a "petition") to the proper court which covers **the county in which you,** the petitioner, **reside.**

Depending on the name by which the court which operates **in your county of residence** is called, the court at which you file may be either the County Court or the Supreme court, or a branch of the Civil Court of the City of New York, if you reside in New York City.

C. Filing a Petition: Some General Instructions to Follow

In this Chapter, we deal with the procedures involved in **one** of the two basic categories of relevance for our purposes—when the party whose name is to be changed is an **ADULT** person, as opposed to a minor. [New York's procedures involving the petition for a minor are set forth in the next chapter, at pp. 45-50]

The procedures, forms and instructions contained in this manual are carefully arranged and organized in a system of orderly "STEPS"—from STEP ONE to STEP EIGHT. In each "STEP", you are told what to do, and when and where necessary, provided with the sample forms along with the related instructions on how to complete or use them.

In processing your name changing petition through the court channels and formalities, or preparing the forms associated with that, you must take the steps **one** (and only one) **at a time,** following the steps **EXACTLY** in the same numerical order in which they are listed below.

D. Step-by-Step Procedures for Filing a Petition
Ready to start the Filing? Simply Follow These Orderly Procedures, Step-by-Step:

Step 1 : FAMILIARIZE YOURSELF WITH THE BASIC BACKGROUND INFORMATION

Familiarize yourself with the minimum prerequisites and conditions for securing the court's approval of a petition, more particularly, those having to do with having the proper reasons or motives for changing one's name. [See Chapters 1 through 3—pp.1-22—especially Chap. 1.]

Step 2 : OBTAIN THE NECESSARY FORMS FOR FILING AN ADULT PETITION

O.K., let's say you are an adult person and you've made the decision. You wish to proceed and actually file to have your name judicially changed. Your next order of business is, of course, to get started: GET THE NECESSARY FILING FORMS.

For the added convenience of our readers,* Do-It-Yourself Legal Publishers makes available to its readership an especially pre-sorted, **standard** all-in-one package of forms meeting your particular State's requirements.

To order the Publisher's package of standard forms, just complete the "Order Form" on p. 111 and send it away to the Publisher's Legal Forms Division listed therein. Simply ask for "New York's Name Change package of forms for an **adult**."

---

* You may, at times, be able to get a supply of the appropriate forms from a local commercial or legal stationery store. As a practical matter, however, most would often carry only a limited or non-appropriate varieties of such forms, and others will have none at all.

Note: Clearly **specify** which of the two basic categories you wish to file under—i.e., for an "adult" or for a "minor". Also, if, by chance, the Petition is not to be filed within the state of New York, say so and specify for what state and locality.

In a New York State filing (they're more or less similar for most other states), you'll typically need such forms as these, or a combination thereof:
(i) Petition for Change of Name (an adult's), with Individual Verification to Petition
(ii) Decree (Order) Granting Change of Name
(iii) Legal Backer Form
(iv) Notice of Petition to the Public
(v) Affidavit of Consent by a Wife or Husband or a Parent (where applicable)
(vi) Affidavit of Service of Notification to Authorities (if applicable)

Step 3 : FILL OUT THE FORMS

Listed below are the illustrative samples of the same forms you shall have obtained. To complete your forms, fill them out in the same way and in the **exact** order in which the forms are listed below.

A good practice when preparing the forms, is to first make Xerox photocopies of the ordered blank forms, and then using a pencil, to complete the photocopies as **"practice rough drafts",** closely following the illustrations and the related instructions outlined in the samples below as you do so. Then, you check the "practice" copies over to make sure that you have everything pretty much in order. Thereafter, using a typewriter, you may then transfer the same information to the original forms that finally get submitted to the court.

THE FORMS ARE NOW LISTED BELOW. COMPLETE THEM IN THE **EXACT** ORDER IN WHICH THEY ARE LISTED HEREIN:

Note: In completing any forms whatsoever, always use the <u>full</u> names on all papers (for the existing as well as for the proposed names); sign all papers in <u>full</u> names, and be consistent all through - same spellings, same signatures, and so on. Write the names in normal order - the last names go last.

1. **"Petition for Change of Name (Adult's)".** [Turn to pp. 35-37 for the sample illustrated preparation of this form.]

2. **"Individual Verification to Petition With The Legal Backer".** [Turn to pp. 38-9 for the sample illustrated preparation of this form.]

Note: Under the format employed in this manual, this form is combined back-to-back with the "Legal Backer" form to make for one single form. They could, alternatively, have been made as two separate forms.

3. **"Decree (Order) Granting Change of Name".** [Turn to pp. 40-1 for the sample illustrated preparation of this form.]

4. "Affidavit of Consent By the Wife/Husband". If it applies. [Turn to p. 42 for the sample illustrated preparation of this form.]

Note: It should be rather obvious that this form will be applicable **only** in situations in which the petitioner is married and the spouse has not "joined" in a single petition. When a petition to change the "family" name - i.e., the family's surname - is involved, then all qualified members of the family (the husband, wife and minor children of 14 to 17 years old) must either "join" in the application by co-signing the petition itself, or give a separate consenting affidavit of the type shown on pp. 57 & 58. Children 18 years of age or older may not join; they many only submit their own individual, separate petitions.

If, by any chance, you run into a situation where your spouse adamantly refuses to grant his/her consent, one thing the court may require you to do is that you give that spouse a formal written notice of the name change anyway. To do so, just fill out a **Notice of Petition to Non-Consenting Parent or Spouse** (p. 59), and simply follow the same procedures outlined under "Step 5" p. 49 to complete the notification process as you would in the case of a non-consenting parent to a minor's application.

5. "Notice of (Filing) Petition" - [Turn to that portion of the Decree within a bracket on p. 41 which is indicated by the pointing arrows therein, for the sample illustrated preparation of this form.] (Note that under the format adopted by a state like New York, this Notice is integrated into the Decree (or Order) Granting a Name Change as an integral part of the said Decree thereof. For most States, however, the format is for a separate form out stands on its own.)

6. "Affidavit of Service of Notification to Authorities", if applicable. Applicable, **only** if petitioner is any of these: an alien, an attorney an ex-convict, and the like. Even if applicable, though, leave out filing out this form for now till you come to "Step 7" (p. 43) below.

Step 4 : SIGN AND NOTARIZE THE APPROPRIATE PAPERS.

Next, you should sign and notarize (or have the appropriate person(s) sign and notarize), at the spots marked "X", the following papers from among the ones you've prepared in STEP 3 above:

(i) The Petition for Change of Name. [To be only **signed** by petitioner, and where change of the "family" name is involved, then also by the spouse and the minor children of at least 14 years of age]

(ii) The Individual Verification [To be **signed** and **notarized** by the same parties as in item #(I) above.]

(iii) Consent Affidavit of the Wife/Husband. [To be **signed** and **notarized** by the proper spouse., if applicable]

How To "Notarize" A Paper

Just in case you don't already know this, what does **"notarizing"** a paper mean? It simply means that you take the paper to a **Notary Public** person and acknowledge in his presence that the contents of the paper are true. You say, in effect, as the Notary Public looks on, "look, I swear that I am the true person who is making the statements contained in this paper and that the statements are true as far as I know." Actually, to notarize a paper, all you'll wind up doing is to sign it in the presence of the Notary Public. Then he'll, in turn, sign the document and put his official stamp to it as evidence that he witnessed you sign it.

Where do you find a Notary Public?

In almost every bank, in some drugstores, stationery stores, lawyers' offices, real estate offices, photocopying shops, check cashing stores, private postal box places, and the like. They are all around you, even in barbershops. Just walk into any of these places and ask for a "Notary Public". Even when a bank or an office does not have one, they would normally direct you to those who do. The current legal charge for notarizing each item in New York State is $1.00

Step 5 : FILE THE PAPERS WITH THE COURT

Now, it's time for you to submit to ("file" with) the court the papers you've prepared. First, though, before you take the papers to the courthouse for filing, you need to properly arrange them.

Here's what you do: first, take the "Legal Backer" sheet and place it on the desk, with the "Verification" part facing upwards and the back of the form facing down to the desk. Now, take the rest of the papers and place them one after the other on top of the Legal Backer in the following order: (I) a "certified" (i.e., officially authenticated) copy of the petitioner's birth certificate (under New York's rules, this is required only if you were born in the state); (ii) a copy of a previous name change court order (of applicable); (iii) Notice of Petition (if any was applicable); and (iv) Consent Affidavit of the Wife/Husband (if applicable). Now, next, place the "Petition for Change of Name" atop of the other papers. Finally, place the "Decree (Order) for Change of Name" at the very top of the heap, facing up so that it (the Decree) is the first in the whole pile to be read. *Now, staple all the forms together to the Legal Backer,* at the top right-hand and left-hand corners of the Legal Backer. [Stapling instructions on how exactly to do this are pre-printed on the Legal Backer form, on the upper part of the Legal Backer.] The papers are finally in shape to be filed with the court.

How, exactly, do you "file" the papers? You simply submit them to the Name Change Court Clerk's desk of that branch of the appropriate court which covers the county or locality in which you live—either the County Court (found in upstate localities), or the Supreme Court, or the Civil Court, if resident in the city of New York.

What happens then? The Name Change clerk will check over the papers you submitted to make sure that they are complete and properly filled out. More often than not, everything will be in order, but don't always count on that happening. If the clerk should tell you there's some necessary information or paper that is missing or improperly filled out, don't even worry about it. To be sure, such 'defective' submissions are just as routine among all filers, more so even among lawyers themselves who are supposedly the all-knowing "experts" in the field! In such instances, simply ask the clerk to tell you **specifically** what and what need to be corrected or supplied. Make a written note of what he says. Then go home, make the corrections or supply the missing documents and resubmit the petition papers.

Assuming the papers you submitted to the clerk are complete and in order, the clerk will endorse his initials on one corner of the petition. Then you'll routinely be required to pay your filing fee to the cashier who'll then assign an **"Index Number"** (also called a **Docket Number"**) to your case. Currently, New York City's fee is $50. (cash or money order) for the Civil Court, or $170 for the Supreme Court. Make sure, from now on, that you enter this number on the face of **each** and **every** paper you submit to the court as this is the only identifying number by which your file is to be traced or preserved in the court records in all future dealings with the court.

Step 6 : ATTEND THE COURT HEARING, IF THERE'S ONE

The exact sequence may slightly vary from one particular court to another. As is equally true in most states in the nation, however, in some New York State jurisdictions, depending on which judge is involved at a given time, a physical appearance of the petitioner may be required before the judge and a formal hearing held thereof. Much more often than not, however—in upwards of 90% of adult petitions involving no contests or objections to the petition—neither the petitioner's physical appearance before the judge, nor a formal court hearing on the petition, will be required of you. Much will depend on the seeming circumstances of your situation. Generally, if it appears to the court clerk (from the contents of the papers you submitted) that your background or petition is neither outrightly outrageous nor seemingly fraudulent or illegal under routine standards of assessment, the clerk will frequently take the liberty to pass the petition on the judge with a favorable recommendation for approval. And the judge will all too likely sign the order to approve it, with no court appearance or hearing required.

In such instances when no court appearance or oral testimony before the judge is required—which is ordinarily the case in the overwhelming majority of adult petitions in New York, as well as in most other courts—all you'll need to do will be to go home after you've submitted the petition papers to the court clerk and paid the filing fees. You shall have inquired from the clerk as to when your petition is scheduled or expected to be read and signed by the judge. You then call the clerk thereafter to see whether the order has been signed. (In some counties, e.g. Kings County, it is often signed the same day, while in others, it could take as much as anywhere from a few days to two weeks or so.)

Granted that, as a practical matter, formal hearings are more the exceptions rather than the rule in adult cases and happen only in far fewer cases— usually when objections are interposed in a given case by a party in interest. Nevertheless, it's still an open possibility that you may be required to have a "hearing" on your petition. If, by chance, you should be required to have a hearing on your petition, though, still you need not sweat over it at all! It's like eating a piece of cake all the same!

Here's what happens in a "hearing" situation:

In essence, in a "hearing" situation, all you'll do differently is that you'll appear on the appointed date before the designated judge at the designated courtroom, and simply present any relevant documents you may have and answer some few questions the judge may ask of you concerning your application. As a rule, the questions asked at such hearings are generally routine and straight forward, in deed, even predictable.

Some Typical Questions Asked At Hearings

Here are some questions the judge may typically ask you (and some possible answers):

Q: Do you truthfully swear that the statements made in this petition (the judge will hold up the petition to you) are true and accurate?

A: Yes.

Q: Why do you want to change your name?

A: (State the same reasons you might have set forth in the petition. See Chapter 1, esp. pp. 1-3   , for the typical reasons for which people often seek a change of name.)

Q: And are those the same grounds or reasons you allege on the petition you submitted to this court?

A: Yes

Q: Is there anyone else with the same or similar name as the one you hereby propose to assume?

A: No.

Q: I gather from your petition that you are presently married with children. Do your spouse and those of your children over 14 years of age, if any, support your proposed change of name?

A: Yes. Your Honor should find annexed to the petition before you a sworn statement of consent from my wife (or husband?) to that effect. None of my children listed in this petition is intended to be affected by this change of name inasmuch as all I seek to change is my first name only. The family last name is not involved here.

Q: Have you ever changed your name before—either judicially or otherwise?

A: No. (If your answer is yes, then give relevant details: when, where and how done, and why?)

Q: Do you have any major debts?

A: No. (If your answer is yes, give a brief listing of the parties' debts to others, for what and of what values or amounts, and for what purposes each debt was incurred.) Most importantly, state whether you listed such debt in your petition and what you've done (or will do), if any, to bring the fact of your change of name to the attention of such creditors).

Q: Do you have any criminal convictions under any name In any jurisdiction in the United States? Or outside the United States?

A: Yes. A total of two convictions, Your Honor, and they are fully listed in the petition you have before you. I have fully served out the terms and sentences on each one and there's nothing currently outstanding against me.

Q: Are there any court cases of any kind (criminal, civil or otherwise) pending anywhere to which you are a party?

A: No. (If yes, you'll have to give the relevant details: name of the case(s), the why, where and wherefore concerning them).

Q: Are you changing your name to conceal any past criminal record, or to escape a legitimate obligation or responsibility you may have?

A: No. I'm not intent on hiding my criminal past, though I do like to put it behind me and move forward. I sent letters (notices) of information about this proposed name change to the Police Commissioner, copy of which you'll find attached to petition papers before you.

Q: Is there anything whatsoever of criminal or anti-social nature from your past, which you are trying to conceal or get away from by changing your name?

A: No, Sir. No illegal, fraudulent or wrongful purposes whatsoever intended sir.

Q: Has anyone raised any objection to your proposed change of name herein?

A: No.

Additional Questions (and Answers) of Relevance in a Minor's Case

Q: Is this petition for a minor person under the age of (say) 18?

A: Yes. (If the answer is yes, then the next several questions may almost certainly apply.)

Q: Is the father (or, as the case may be, the mother) joining in this petition or otherwise consenting to the proposed change of the child's name?

A: No. (If the answer is yes, than all you need further do is to offer the consenting parent's sworn statement ["affidavit"] of consent and that issue shall have been almost settled.)

Q: Why not?

A: The father has practically abandoned the child, your honor. The child is now 10 years of age. And not once, since she was a month old, has the supposed father even come around to see her, or ever contributed anything for her support, schooling, medical care, clothing, housing, feeding, you name it. I even tried taking him to Family Court in 19____ to get some kind of child support from the man. But he ignored the court's order of support and swore he was never going to pay. Not to speak of the fact that he never comes to see the child and has in no way shown any king of parental interest in this child.

Q: In what way, if any, can you see this change working out in the child's own best interest?

A: The only person the child has ever known as the real father in her life has been her stepfather, Mr._____. He's been the one who has done everything a true father is supposed to do for the child—caring, love, support, everything. To change the child's name so that she takes after her stepfather's last name, would further strengthen those bonds of love, common identity, sharing and family between the daughter and father.

Q: Was the natural father given a formal written notice, anyway, about this petition?

A: Yes. (Elaborate on the nature and timing of the notice given, how given, and any response or feedback you got from the parent in question, if any.)

Q: Is the child, the object of this petition, 14 years of age or over?

A: Yes. (If the answer is no, then the next set of questions may not apply.)

Q: And is she in court today? What has she herself got to say for herself about all this?

A: She's in court and can speak to the petition if your Honor wants her to or so directs.

[The child herself (himself) may probably be called to come before the judge to testify at this juncture]

What happens after the matter has come before the judge?

The judge, after having reviewed the substance of your petition—whether after having had a hearing on it, or without one at all—will in all likelihood thereafter put his signature to the papers in approval of your application to assume another name. (In order for him to deny your (adult) petition, he would have had to have a "substantial reason"* to show for that. That's what the law says!)

---

*See p.10

Step  : PUBLISH IN NEWSPAPER A NOTICE OF THE NAME CHANGE ORDER; THEN, WHERE APPLICABLE, SEND NOTICE OF THE CHANGE TO REQUIRED AUTHORITIES,

Upon the judge approving your petition, he (or she) will sign the original **"Decree or Order Granting Change of Name"** form—one of those papers you had submitted to the court clerk when you filed the petition.

Now, here is what you have to do:

1. After having filed your petition with the court clerk, or, if one is required, after having had your hearing before the judge, you should **make sure** that you make it a point to call the name change court clerk constantly thereafter (every day or two) to see when the papers are signed. This way, you would be in a position to follow up the remainder of the procedures promptly on a **timely** basis.

2. Go to the courthouse **without delay** as soon as the Decree (order) Granting Change of Name is signed by the judge. Ask the Name Change Clerk for the signed order in your court file, and make at least two (maybe more) Xerox photocopies of that order.

3. Look at the space provided for it in the text of the Order; the judge shall have entered in that space the name of the particular newspaper(s) he picks in which the **Notice of Filing Petition** is required to be published. *Now, **without delay**, you should have send away one copy of the photocopy of the signed Order to the specific newspaper(s) designated in the order.* (You may look up the newspaper's address and phone number by simply looking in the Telephone Book). Attach a check to cover the newspaper's quoted charge for the publication.

     The newspaper will select out from the Order that portion of the order constituting a Notice which is meant to be published (see the portion indicated by arrows on p. 41) and that's the part the newspaper publishes for a New York filing).

4. Now, if you (the party whose name is being changed) are any of the following: an alien, an attorney, or one with record of prior criminal convictions, you will have to formally serve a notice of the change of name upon the appropriate authorities, as outlined below.

(a) For An Alien:
You send, by Certified Mail and without delay, one photocopy of the signed order to: District Director, U.S. Immigration and Naturalization Service, 26 Federal Plaza, New York, N.Y. 10007.

(b) For An Attorney:

You send, by Certified Mail and without delay, one photocopy of the signed order to: The Clerk of the Appellate Division of whatever the Department is to which the petitioner was admitted to bar.

(c) For One with Prior Convictions:

You send, by Certified Mail and without delay, one photocopy of the signed order to: The Division of Criminal Justice Services, Executive Park Tower, Stuyvesant Plaza, Albany, N.Y. 12203.

5.   Thereafter, for **each** of the above notifications you may have made, if any, the petitioner must next make out a written statement certifying that such notification had actually been given, and then file this statement with the court clerk within a specific period, as stipulated in the signed Judge's Order—usually within 20 days from the date of the signing of the order.

Here's what you do to fulfil this requirement. Just complete the form on p. 43 titled, **"Affidavit of Service of Notification to Authorities"**, sign and **notarize** it, and promptly file it with the court clerk.

6.   Let's say that, in the meantime, the newspaper has now completed the publication of the Notice of Name Change (item #3 above). The Newspaper will return to you a document titled, **"Affidavit of Publication"**—simply, a sworn statement by the newspaper by which its publishers certify that they had, in fact, done the required publication. (See a sample copy of this document on p. 44). Now, all you do is this: take this document, the Affidavit of Publication, and go and file it with the court clerk just as urgently.

7.   The appropriate court clerk (usually the Records Certification clerk, this time), will, upon your paying a "certification" fee (it's $5 or $4 in New York), issue you the final, "certified" (i.e., stamped and confirmed by the court clerk as genuine) copy of the Order Granting Change of Name. With this final, certified copy of the Order in hand, you are just about done. That's the "official" document you need to present anywhere to show that you had a "legal" change of name!

Step 8 : NOW, GET YOUR NEW NAME RECOGNIZED IN "OFFICIAL" CIRCLES.

Sure, you've completed the process of formally changing your name legally, alright. But, don't assume that that alone, in and of itself, automatically establishes the recognition or acceptance of your new name with everyone or every authority that may count in your life. Not at all! The fact is, changing your name even "legally," is one thing; having the new name accepted or established "socially" in official and non-official circles, is quite another thing.

What this means is that there's one further extra step that needs to be taken to truly, finally, complete the job—essentially the task of informing and bringing your new legal name to the attention and official recognition of the key institutions, people and governmental authorities that matter.

Here's how you may inform some of the authorities that often come into play in most people's lives:

The Post Office:

Go to your local post office. Ask them to list you at your address in **both** your old names and new ones. This way, you can be sure of not having to miss your mail.

Social Security:

Go to your local Social Security office and ask to fill out an OAAN-7003 form ("Request for change in Social Security Records") stating that you've legally assumed a new name.

Income Tax Authorities:

As to the federal tax, the Form OAAN-7003 you filled out with the Social Security office shall have been automatically forwarded to the IRS, hence you probably need not make any further independent effort to inform the IRS. As to the state and local income tax authorities, simply send a brief letter to the Taxpayer Service Division of the locality's central office informing them of your new name. Don't forget to indicate your usual social security number.

Driving license, Car registration, Welfare authorities, and the like.

Take a certified copy of the Court's "Order Granting Change of Name" to the local office and have them put your records under your new name.

Birth Certificate

Send a **certified** copy of the court's "Order Granting Change of Name" to your state of birth's Bureau of Vital Statistics office (it's at 125 Worth Street in Manhattan, for a New York City resident), with a brief letter of explanation attached. They will either issue you another birth certificate in your new name (for a fee), or merely make an official notation of your change of name on the birth certificate.

Your credit card companies, other creditors, your utility or insurance companies, schools, colleges, etc.

Simply send a simple I-have-legally-changed-my-name letter of notification to each stating your old and new names.

Your banks and other financial institutions.

Take your **certified** court order to them and have new signature cards signed in your new name for your accounts.

Passport Office

Take your **certified** court order there and fill out a passport application or amendment form. You'll receive a passport under your new name.

(Adult Petition—New York)

(Enter the details)

The _____*Civil*_____ Court of the State/City of _____*New York*_____
In and for the County of _____*Kings*_____ State of _____*New York*_____ .

Re: Matter of the Application of
(Petitioner's present name, in full)
for Petitioner to Assume Another
Name as: **(Proposed name, in full)**

Index No. (enter this)
PETITION FOR
CHANGE OF
NAME (ADULT'S)

I (we), the undersigned person (or persons), being duly sworn, depose and say:

1. I am (we are) the petitioner(s) herein; and I am (we are) an adult person over the age of 18.

2. Petitioner(s) reside at this address: [***petitioner's home address?***] _____ located in the city of _____ , County of _____ , State of _____ , and has (have) resident in this state for the past _____ months/years prior to filing this petition.

3. This is an application to seek the Court's approval to change petitioner's present name, which is, [***petitioner's present name, in full***] _____ to another name, namely, [***name proposed to be assumed in full***] _____ .

4. Petitioner was born on the _____ day of _____ 19_____, in the city of _____ county of _____ , state of _____ ; and said petitioner is currently a citizen of _____ by birth/naturalization,* and has been such a citizen for at least six months prior to the submission of this application. Attached hereto is petitioner's birth certificate [OR, a certified transcript of his/her birth certificate, OR a certificate of discharge from the Army] showing his/her date and place of birth.

5. Petitioner is _____, years of age.

6. The grounds and reasons for which this change of name is being sought, are as follows:

[*Set forth here the reasons for which you want the name changed*]

EXAMPLE, (say it has to do with need to eliminate a business or professional
            disadvantage):

This Petitioner (or Petitioners) is a professional entertainer for a theatre and stage actor, and a surname that is shorter, and which can be easily pronounced, spelled and remembered by the public and associates alike, would be substantially advantageous to this petitioner is his career prospects and growth.

OR

*Petitioner's present surname, which is [**enter it here in full**] is difficult for many Americans to pronounce, is frequently mispronounced and misspelled, and, as a result, is difficult for them to remember. Many professional contacts petitioner made have been lost by him as agents and associates have often been unable to find petitioner's name in the telephone directory and are often embarrassed for mispronouncing or misspelling petitioner's name.*

    *Hence, petitioner wishes to assume the surname proposed here, namely, [**the proposed surname, in full**?] inasmuch as the proposed new surname is easier to pronounce or to spell or remember in the American environment, and would be to petitioner's better professional image and advantage.*

---

* Strike out one or the other word or phrase   Page 1 of 3

(ADULT PETITION—NEW YORK)

7. Petitioner(s) has not been convicted of any crimes or adjudicated a bankrupt by any court or jurisdiction; except: None

[If, on the other hand, you have been convicted of a crime or been adjudicated a bankrupt, then simply say so and give the bare essentials of the facts—e.g., what the crimes were, the courts where handled, their dispositions by the courts, whether you've served out the imposed sentence or paid the fine, as applicable, etc.]

8. There are no major debts, no judgements or liens of record now outstanding against petitioner; except: None

[If **however**, such are basically applicable to you, then just set forth the essential details, instead—what major debts are owned or the liens involved, names of the creditors or lienors, and the like]

9. No court actions or proceedings are now pending against petitioner, or against any property in petitioner's name.

[If otherwise, however, then set forth the details her, instead, listing what cases are pending, in what court they are so pending, the nature of the case, etc.]

10. No bonds or commercial papers are outstanding against me.

[If otherwise, however, then set forth the details here, instead.]

11. Petitioner's occupation/employment is as follows : _____

[Set forth the occupation, trade or profession; where employed, if any, and how long there.]

12. Petitioner's marital status is as follows: single and never been married.

[If, however, you are married (or divorced), then set forth the facts here, instead (the name of your spouse, the names and ages of the minor children in the marriage, if any]

13. Petitioner desires also that the spouse and minor children, as named above, be included in this application, that their surnames, only, be changed from its present, to _____.

[If this is a "family" type petition whereby the change of name, usually of the surname, is to cover the whole family (the both parents as well as the minor children), then you must so specify that fact here and attach each party's birth certificate and affidavit of consent, if applicable]

14. Petitioner avers that the proposed change of name is not sought for illegal or fraudulent purposes or evil intent, or to delay or hinder creditors; that no person will in any way be injured or adversely affected, nor the legitimate rights thereof prejudiced or infringed upon, by the proposed change of name herein.

(ADULT PETITION—NEW YORK)

15.   No application has been previously filed by or for petitioner in any court or jurisdiction for the name change matter proposed herein; except: <u>None.</u>
[If otherwise, however, then state the applicable facts, instead—in what court such previous petition had been filed, when so filed, and whether or not the court approved it, and the reasons cited, etc.

***WHEREFORE,** Petitioner prays the court to grant this application, authorizing the petitioner to assume the proposed name, namely: *(the proposed name of petitioner, in full,)*_____, inasmuch as the proposed change of name would be beneficial to petitioner, and to his/her best interests and welfare, and is not intended for any fraudulent or wrongful purpose, or to interfere with the legitimate rights of others in any way.

(Date on which
signed & notarized)

Signed: *[Petitioner's original names, in full]*
(Petitioner)

Dated, this _____

day of _____, 19_____

Full Name (Print) _____
Address:_____

---

* **USE THIS CLAUSE, INSTEAD, WHEN YOUR STATE'S PROCEDURES EMPLOY ORDER TO-SHOW-CAUSE METHOD:**
"WHEREFORE, petitioner prays the court to sign an Order to Show Cause designating a specified date and place at which cause is to be shown why this application for change of name should not be granted; and, that upon a hearing, the court make an order authorizing petitioner herein to assume the proposed name, namely; **(the proposed name, in full)**, in as much as the proposed change of name would be beneficial to petitioner, and petitioner herewith swears that it is not intended for any fraudulent or wrongful purpose, or to interfere with the legitimate rights of others in any way."

38

Individual Verification
To Petition

Index No. (Enter This)

STATE OF_____,

COUNTY OF _____ ss.:

   I/We **(*Petitioners' Present Name, in full*)** , being duly sworn, say: I am (we are) the **PETITIONER** in the within case or matter; I (we) have read the foregoing/annexed document, titled the **PETITION FOR CHANGE OF NAME** , and know the contents thereof; the same is true of my (our) own knowledge, except as to the matters therein stated to be alleged on information and belief, and as to those matters I (we) believe them to be true.

Sworn to before me on the _____
day of _____ 19 _____.

SIGNED: **(*Petitioner sign present, full name*)**
The name signed must be printed beneath

SIGNED: **(*Second Petitioner, if any, signs*)**
name signed must be printed beneath

_____
(Notary Public)

My commission Expires:

_____19_____.

(Fold this Backer Here)↘

IN THE

Index No. _____ Year 19 ____

COURT OF THE CITY/STATE OF _____

FOR The COUNTY/DISTRICT OF _____

PETITION TO CHANGE NAME,

FROM: ....

TO: ....

ORDER/Petition for
Change Of Name

FILED BY:

Address: _____

_____ , Petitioner pro se;

"Legal Backer" form

(Get the Judge's name
from the clerk)

PRESENT:
Hon._____
Justice/Judge

_____
Re: Application of:
[Enter] **(adult petitioner's name, in full)**
To Assume Another Name as:
(the proposed name, in full)

(Enter These)

At the **(name of court)**, Court of the
City/State of _____ held in
and for the County of _____, at the
county's courthouse thereof, on the _____day
of _____19_____.

ORDER/DECREE GRANTING CHANGE OF NAME (ADULT'S)

Index/File No. (enter this)

Upon reading the Verified Petition of **(petitioner's present names, in full)** _____
presented this day before me requesting leave of this Court for the petitioner herein to assume
another name, viz: **(petitioner's proposed name, in full)** _____ in
place of his present name; (and, after hearing)**,and upon reviewing the supporting Affidavit(s),
birth certificate and/or other evidence presented herewith in proof and support of the petitioner's
application thereof; and it appearing that the allegations in the Verified Petition are true, and that
the petitioner is a citizen of **(enter it)** _____, by birth/naturalization*, and was born in the
city of _____, County of_____, state of _____, on
the _____ day of the month of _____ 19 _____, bearing Birth Certificate No.
(enter B.C. #, if any) _____; [and it being noted by the court that petitioner is
married to **(full name of wife)** _____the wife, and that the couple
has_____ children from the marriage, named and ages as follows:
(names of each child, in full, and date of birth thereto) _____
and that each person desires and/or consents to assume the proposed surname herein)**; and it
further appearing that there is no reasonable objection to the proposed change of name, and that
the proposed change of name is not for any fraudulent or wrongful purpose, or offensive to
common decency and good taste, and will not prejudice or adversely affect the legitimate interests
of others;

Exclude or strike
out clause about
marriage/children
if not applicable.

NOW WHEREFORE, after due deliberations on the application herein, it is

ORDERED, that **(petitioner's present names, in full)** _____, petitioner, is
authorized to assume the proposed name as **(proposed new names, in full**_____**)**, in place
and stead of the present name, effective from the _____ day of _____19____, upon the
petitioner complying with the provisions of this order, as follows:

(Clerk fills in)

_____
* Strike out one or the other word or phrase
**Exclude the clause (enclosed within the bracket). If not applicable in terms of your circumstances.

(ADULT ORDER—NEW YORK)

First, that this Order and the petition and all supporting papers upon which this order is granted, be entered in the Office of the Clerk of this court within 10 days from the date hereof; and second, that within 20 days from the date of entry of this order, a Notice of this order be published, once in this newspaper:___**(Court fills in**___**),** the said notice to read substantially as follows:

(newspaper to be designated by the court)

(obtain from court)

NOTICE is hereby given that an order entered by the __**(name of court)**__ Court, __**(enter)**__ county, on the _____day of _____19 _____, bearing the index Number __**(enter)**____, a copy of which may be examined at the office of the clerk, located at __**(address of court where petition is filed)**_____ in Room __**(get this from the clerk),**__ grants me the right, effective from the _____ day of _____ 19 ____, to assume the name of **(the proposed new name in full)**_____. My present address is __**(enter)**_____; the date of my birth is __**(enter)**_____ at _____**(City & State)**; my present name is: **(set forth, in full)**_____.

(Piece to be sent to Newspaper for Publication)

(Clerk fills in, as appropriate)

and, third, that thereafter, within __40__ days from the date of this Order; proof of the said publication shall, by affidavit, be filed and recorded in the office of the clerk of this court; and

that thereafter, namely, after the foregoing directives are complied with, the said petitioner shall be known as __**(the proposed new names, in full)**_____on and from the above specified effective date, and by no other name;

and Mrs **(name of spouse)**_____, the wife of petitioner, shall be known as __**(new name, in full)**__ and by no other name, her surname being likewise changed, and the said minor children, namely, **(list them, in full**_____**),** shall be known as __**(list new names, in full)**_____ respectively, their surname being similarly changed, all effective on and from the date heretofore specified above.*

Leave blank.

ENTER:__**(Judge to sign here)**__
JUDGE

*****NOTE:** If petitioner is either an alien, or an ex-convict (see explanation given in pp.32-33), then you may provide herein an additional paragraph to that effect, as follows:

Clause for Alien
    and it is further ORDERED, that a copy of this Order be served by Certified Mail, upon the U.S. Immigration and Naturalization Service at *(address)*, within 10 days of the entry of this order, and that proof of such service be filed with the clerk of the court herein within 10 days thereafter.

Clause for prior criminal conviction
    and it is further ORDERED, that a copy of this Order be served upon the Head, Division of Criminal Justice Service of this state, at *(address)*, within 10 days of the entry of this order, and that proof of such service be filed with the clerk of the court herein within 10 days thereafter.

42

Index No. **(Enter this # from the Court Clerk)**

AFFIDAVIT OF CONSENT BY WIFE/HUSBAND

(State & County
where paper is
notarized)

State of _____

County of _____ ss:

I, the undersigned person, being duly sworn, respectfully declare and say:

That I am over 18 years of age, and reside at this address: **(consenting party's address)**
_____. That I am the husband/wife/guardian* of the adult petitioner, **(the present name of the petitioner in full)** _____, who was born on the _____ day of _____, 19 _____, in the city/town of _____, county and state of _____. _____← (enter these facts)

That a PETITION by the said petitioner to legally change his/her* name is being filed in Court by the above-named petitioner, the object being to change his/her name from the present name, as given above, to another name, namely: **(enter, in full, the proposed new name)** _____.

I have fully read the said petition, and I hereby give my consent voluntarily to the proposed change of name, and assert no objection whatsoever to the petitioner's application thereof.

Signed: **(Consenting Person signs here)**   **(SPOUSE)**

Name Signed, printed in full:_____.

(to be filled
in by the
Notary Public)

Before me, a duly qualified Notary Public of the State of _____, appeared Mr./Mrs. _____, to me known, or made known to me to be the individual described in the within instrument who signed, acknowledged and swore to this instrument as true, on this _____ day of _____ 19 _____.

_____
(Notary Public)

* Cross out the inapplicable word or term.

Index No. **(enter this)**

Re: In the Matter of the Application by
(petitioner's present name in full) to
Change the Name of **(minor adult's present
name in full)** a Minor/Adult, to this
Name: **(the proposed new name in full)** .

AFFIDAVIT OF SERVICE OF
NOTIFICATION TO AUTHORITIES

State of _____ County of _____ ss.:

**(enter date when
you mailed paper
to the authorities.)**

Mr./Mrs./Ms. **(Petitioner's old name in full)** , being duly sworn deposes and
says: that he/she is the adult petitioner herein; that on the _____ day
of _____19___, he served the within document(s), namely, **(specify which document)**
_____, upon this person/authority **(enter name of the party served)** by mailing,
by Certified Mail, a true copy of the same document(s) securely enclosed in a post-paid
wrapper in the Post Office—a Branch Post Office—regularly maintained by the United
States Government. The said mail was addressed to the said person/authority as follows:
(set forth the address) , which is the address previously designated by
the party for that purpose, or the last known residence or place where said party then kept
an office, between which places there then was and now is a regular communication by
mail.

(Sign old name)
Signed: *(Petitioner signs here - in presence of the Notary Public)*
(Adult Petitioner)

Address:_____

Sworn to before me, on this _____

day of _____19_____

_____
(Notary Public)

AFFIDAVIT OF PUBLICATION

Brooklyn Record

44 COURT STREET
Brooklyn, N. Y.

(718) 875-8230 .

State of New York }
County of Kings, City of New York
Borough of Brooklyn } ss:

CHARLES RICHMAN, , of the Borough of Brooklyn, in the City of New York, being duly sworn, says that he is the publisher of the Brooklyn Record, a newspaper published in the County of Kings, Borough of Brooklyn, City of New York, and that the Notice, of which the annexed is a true copy, has been published in said newspaper once each week for .... weeks, successively, commencing on the ____12____ day of _____Dec_____,19__ and the following days:

FILE
SPECIAL 2 TERM
DEC 2 2 1986
CIVIL COURT
KINGS COUNTY

LEGAL NOTICE

Notice is hereby given that an order entered by the Civil Court, Kings County on the 4 day of Dec,1986,bearing Index No.N-708/1986, a copy of which may be examined at the office of the Clerk,located at 141 Livingston St.,Brooklyn,N.Y. in Room 304,grants me the right, effective on the 13 day of Jan. 1987 to assume the name of SHEM YAQUOB.Present address is 1117 Flatbush Ave., Brooklyn,N.Y.;date of birth is March 14, 1963;place of birth is Trench Town,Jamaica,W.I. Present name is Anglo Oscar Johnson.

Copy of the notice that is published by the newspaper

SWORN TO AND SUBSCRIBED BEFORE ME

THIS.....1ᵞ.....DAY OF....Dec,1986

MARIE J. DUFFY
Notary Public, State of New York
No. 43-4654789
Qualified in Richmond County
Commission Expires March 30, 19 87

NOTARY PUBLIC.

CHAPTER 5

NEW YORK'S NAME CHANGE PROCEDURES: CHANGING THE NAME OF A MINOR CHILD

As was amply elaborated in the preceding Chapter 1 (see Section E thereby at pp. 7-9), one basic differentiation of relevance in court proceedings for name change, relates to the issue of whether the object of the name change is an **adult,** on the one hand, or a **minor,** on the other hand. In the preceding Chapter 4 (p. 23), we dealt with the details of New York's name change procedures in terms of the **"adult"** situation—that is, when a person over 18 years of age in New York as well as most states, is the object of the petition. **In this present chapter, we shall deal, on the other hand, with the parallel procedures involved when the object of the name change application is a "minor" or "infant" person (generally, a person under 18 years of age).**

A. Who May File a Petition and Where

As is equally true with adult-type petitions, New York state's rules relating to change of name for minor persons follow a rather general principle that are common to most states. Under these rules, the key factor which differentiates a minor's petition from an adult's basically boils down to the matter of requiring some adult party's consent before you may change a minor's name.

More specifically, most states (New York included) strictly require that the petition to change the name of a minor person (also called and "infant"), may not be made directly by the child himself, but by some adult third party—the minor's parent or parents, legal guardian, next friend, and the like—who is to act for and on the minor's behalf. Both parents of the minor, if surviving, may join in the petition. However, the rules permit a single parent who, for one reason or the other, finds it impossible to win the consent or cooperation of the other parent, to proceed alone.

As with adult petitions, the minor's petition is formally filed by an (adult) resident of the state, in that branch of the proper court covering the country of one's residence—the County Court, or Supreme Court, or a branch of the Civil Court of the City of New York, depending on which court operates in the particular county of one's residence.

B. Filing a Minor's Petition: Some General Instructions to Follow

The procedures, forms, and instructions contained in this manual are carefully arranged and organized in a system of orderly "STEPS" - from STEP ONE to STEP EIGHT. In each "STEP", you are told what to do, and, when and where necessary, provided with the sample forms along with the related instructions on how to complete or use them.

In processing your petition through the court channels and formalities, or preparing the forms associated with that, you must take the steps **one** (and only one) **at a time**, following the steps **EXACTLY** in the same numerical order in which they are listed below.

C. Step-by-Step Procedures for Filing a Petition For A Minor

Ready to start filling? Simply follow these orderly procedures, step-by-step:

Step 1 : FAMILIARIZE YOURSELF WITH THE BASIC BACKGROUND INFORMATION

First, familiarize yourself with the minimum prerequisites and conditions for securing the court's approval of a petition to change a minor person's name, more particularly, those having to do with securing the necessary adult consent and the proper reasons or motives for which such a change may be sought.
(Refer to Chapters 1 & 3 (pp. 1 & 18) of the manual, with particular attention to pp. 2-3,8-10 & 19,thereof.)

Note: One point that should be added at this point, and rather emphatically, is this: in virtually every name change situation involving a minor, a central, probably controlling consideration revolves around the issue of whether or not the consent or blessing of certain **"interested persons"** - notably the minor's living parent(s) or, in the absence of that, his legal guardian or custodian— are forthcoming in support of the proposed name change. The centrality of this can hardly be over emphasized. To put it rather directly, then, one thing you had rather done at this juncture before you proceed any further, is this: **begin now, if you have not already done so, to seek out the "interested persons" in the minor's life as well as their whereabouts; and turn on all that charming powers of persuasion at your disposal to win their consent,** or, at least, their passive acquiesence, to the proposal!

Step 2 : OBTAIN THE NECESSARY FORMS FOR FILING A MINOR'S PETITION

O.K. Let's say the decision has been made. You are to file a court petition to change the name of a minor person—one who is under 18 years of age under New York state's and most other states' rules. Your next order of business is, of course, to get started: GET THE NECESSARY FILING FORMS. How do you get a supply of the appropriate forms?

For the added convenience of our readers,* Do-It-Yourself Legal Publishers makes available to its readership an especially pre-sorted, **standard** all-in-one package of forms meeting to your particular state's requirements.

To order the Publisher's package of standard forms, just complete the "Order Form" on p. 111 and send it away to the Publisher's Legal Forms Division address listed therein. Simply ask for "New York's Name Change package of forms for a **minor.**" (For filers requiring forms for states other than New York, see the Order Form in Appendix F.)

---

* You may, at times, be able to get a supply of the appropriate forms from a local commercial or legal stationery store. As a practical matter, however, most would often carry only a limited or non-appropriate varieties of such forms, and others will have none at all.

Step 3 : FILL OUT THE FORMS

Illustrative samples of the exact forms you will need - and for which you shall have received blank copies from the Publisher, upon an order—are listed below. To complete your forms, fill them out in the same way and in the **exact** order in which the forms are listed below.

A good practice when preparing the forms, is to first make a Xerox photocopy of the ordered blank forms, and then using a pencil, to complete the Xerox photocopies first as **"practice rough draft",** closely following the illustrations and the related instructions outlined in the samples below as you go about it. Then, you should check the "practice" copies over to make sure that you have everything pretty much in order. Thereafter, using a typewriter, you may then transfer the same information to the original forms that finally get submitted to the court.

THE FORMS ARE NOW LISTED BELOW. (COMPLETE THEM IN THE **EXACT** ORDER IN WHICH THEY ARE LISTED HEREIN):

<u>Note:</u>   In completing any forms whatsoever, always use the <u>full</u> names on all papers (for existing as well as for the proposed names); sign all papers in <u>full</u> names, and be consistent all through - same spellings, same signatures, and so on. Write the names in normal order - the last names go last.

1.   **"Petition for Change of Name (Minor's)".** [Turn to pp. 51-3 for the sample illustrated preparation of this forms]

2.   **"Individual Verification to Petition"** with the "Legal Backer". [Turn to pp. 54 for the sample illustrated preparation of this form]. **NOTE:** Under the format employed in this manual, this form is combined, front-and-back, with the "Legal Backer" form to make for one single form. They could, alternatively, have been made as two separate forms.

3.   **"Decree/Order Granting Change of Name (minor's) ".** [Turn to pp. 55-6 for the sample illustrated preparation of this form.]

4.   **"Affidavit of Consent of Minor's Parent(s) or Guardian(s)"** [Turn to pp. 57 for the sample illustrated preparation of this form.]

> Note: This form is to be prepared and given to the minor's parent(s) or guardian(s) for their signatures in situations where such parent(s) or guardians have not already "joined" in (i.e., signed) the petition itself. Remember, further, that minors of 14 to 17 years of age are required to "join" in the petition by either singing it along with the petitioning party, or giving a separate consenting affidavit of the type shown for form item #5 below.

5.   **"Affidavit of Minor's Consent in Support of Petition"** – applicable, <u>only</u> when the minor is <u>over</u> certain age levels, as, say, 14 years of age or over. [Turn to p. 58 for the sample illustrated preparation of this form.]

6. **"Notice of Petition to the Public"** [Turn to that portion of the Decree within a bracket on p. 56 which is indicated by the pointing arrows therein, for the sample illustrated preparation of this form.]

> (Note, however, that in the format employed in this manual, this Notice is integrated into the Decree Granting a Name Change as an integral part of the said degree thereof. Under a slightly different format used by some other jurisdictions, however, the form is set apart and stands separately by itself.)

7. **"Notice of Petition to Non-Consenting Parent (or spouse)",** if necessary. [Turn to p. 59 for sample illustrated preparation of this form.]

> **NOTE:** This form will be applicable **only** when there exists a situation where one or both of the minor's parents refuse to grant their written consent, which will then mean that you'll need to give that non-consenting parent (or guardian) a formal written notice of your filing the petition anyway. The actual mechanics of physically giving this notice are outlined under "STEP 5" on p. 49.

8. **"Affidavit of Service of Notification to Authorities",** if applicable. [sample of form is on p. 60]. Would be applicable **only** if the minor is any of these: an alien, an attorney, an ex-convict, and the like. Even if applicable, though, leave out filling out this form for now till you are in "STEP 7" below.

Step 4 : SIGN AND NOTARIZE THE APPROPRIATE PAPERS

Next, you (the adult persons acting as the petitioners) should sign and notarize, at the spots marked "X", the following papers you've prepared in "STEP 3" above:

(i) The Petition for Change of Name. [To be only **signed** by the petitioning adult or adults. However, where the minor himself is at least 14 years of age, he himself must sign (and, where that is also called for, notarize) the papers as well.]

(ii) The Individual Verification. [To be **signed** and **notarized** by the petitioning adults, and also by the minor as well, if he/she is at least 14 years of age]

(iii) Consent Affidavit of Parent/Guardian in Support of Petition. [To be **signed** and **notarized** by the non-petitioning parent or guardian]

(iv) Affidavit of Minor's Consent in Support of Petition, when employed. [To be **signed** and **notarized** by the over-14 minor]

(v) Notice of Petition to Non-Consenting Parent (or Spouse). [To be only **signed** by the petitioning adult, assuming that there arises the need to use the form, in the first place. For the kinds of situation for which the use of this form may be called for, see the second paragraph of "STEP 5" below]

How to "Notarize a Paper"
Just in case you don't already know this, **what does "NOTARIZING" a paper mean?** If, by chance, you have any problem about this, please turn to "STEP 4" of the previous Chapter 4 at (p. 27), for the information on that outlined therein.

Step 5 : FILE THE PAPERS WITH THE COURT

[See the procedures and instructions outlined for the adult-type petition in "STEP 5" of Chapter 4, at pp. 27-8, and simply follow here those same procedures.] All references therein to such terms as "petitioner", or "adult", should obviously be changed accordingly to reflect the applicable equivalent for a minor-type petition, e.g., the "Consent Affidavit of the Wife/Husband", should mean the "Consent Affidavit of the Minor's Parent", and so on]

What happens, though, when one is confronted with a situation wherein the minor's guardian or the other parent would not cooperate or give his consent to a proposed change of name? Does that mean that such a petition is automatically doomed and there's no further remedy available to a petitioner? Not at all! Quite to the contrary, the rules of most states are careful to provide ways for making allowance for such a problem and clearing the way for moving on with the name changing proceedings anyway.

Here, for example, is what you do in such a situation under New York's rules: You are to go ahead and give a formal written notice of the proposed name change application to the non-consenting parent, anyway.* To do so, you'll simply consult with the Name Change Clerk to get the appropriate court calendar dates on which to schedule a hearing, and, using that, you fill out the NOTICE OF PETITION TO NON-CONSENTING PARENT, a sample copy of which is reproduced on p. 59. You send a copy of this notice to the non-consenting party by Certified mail, and then submit to the Court Clerk the original copy of the notice along with the receipt of the certified mail, attached.

Step 6 : ATTEND THE COURT HEARING, IF THERE'S ONE

[See the procedures and instructions outlined for court hearing in the adult-type petition in "STEP 6" of Chapter 4, at pp. 28-30, and simply follow here those same procedures.]

NOTE: There are a few points of departure in respect to the minor's case: (I) the minor-type petitions are more likely than not to require a hearing, especially when a parent or guardian actively interposes an objection to the application; (ii) the primary object of interest to the court in such a hearing is the **minor's own** needs and circumstances, what his 'best interests' seemingly are, and whether such will be better served, or ill-served, by a change; (iii) a minor whose age is within a certain upper bracket (from 14 to 17 years old in New York, for example), would have to make the court appearance as well, if a hearing is held.

---

* The primary object for which this requirement is made, apparently, is to properly inform a person with some probable interest in such matter about the fact of what is going on thereby affording him, at the very least, the opportunity to either challenge and be heard on the matter, or to let it go unchallenged. Whatever he chooses to do, one way or the other at that point, shall have at least been his own choice.

Step  : **PUBLISH IN NEWSPAPER A NOTICE OF THE NAME CHANGE ORDER; THEN, WHERE APPLICABLE, SEND NOTICE OF THE CHANGE TO REQUIRED AUTHORITIES.**

Upon the judge approving the petition to have the minor child's name changed, the judge will sign the original Decree or Order Granting Change of Name—one of those papers you had submitted to the court clerk when you filed the petition.

And what follows next? [Please turn to the procedures and instructions outlined for the adult-type situation in "STEP 7" of Chapter 4, at pp. 32-3, and simply follow here those same procedures there, taking care to eliminate those aspects that are probably inapplicable in a minor-type situation (e.g., having to notify the authorities as an attorney or a person with past criminal records, as in under item #4 on p. 32-3)]

Also, if the minor whose name is being changed falls under any of the relevant categories for which notification of the authorities is required (e.g., an alien, an attorney, or an ex-convict, etc.), then further turn to Item #'s 4 & 5 on p. 32-3, and simply do exactly the same things as are outlined therein in an adult petition.

Step 8 : **NOW, GET THE NEW NAME RECOGNIZED IN "OFFICIAL" CIRCLES**

[See the procedures and instructions outlined in "STEP 8" of Chapter 4, on p. 33 above, and follow here those same procedures there (except, of course, those aspects that are clearly inapplicable for a minor.)]

Minor's Petition—New York

(Enter the details)

IN THE ___*Civil*___ COURT OF THE STATE/CITY OF ___*New York*___,
IN AND FOR THE COUNTY OF ___*Kings*___, STATE OF ___*New York*___.

Re: Matter of the Application of __(adult Petitioner's Name)__
to change the Name of __(Minor's present name, in full)__, A
Minor, to the Name: __(proposed name of minor, in full)__

Case/Index No._____

PETITION FOR CHANGE
OF NAME (Minor's)

I (we), the undersigned person (persons), being duly sworn, depose and say:

1. I am (we are) an adult person over the age of 18, and am (we are), the petitioner(s) in this matter.

2. Petitioner(s) reside at this address: [petitioner's home address?] _____ , located in the city of _____, county of _____, state of_____, and has (have) resided in this state for the past _____months/years prior to filing this petition.

(Enter the details as applicable.

3. This petition (application) is being filed for and on behalf of __(minor's present name, in full)__ _____, a MINOR, to seek the courts' authorization for the said minor to assume another name, namely: __(proposed name of minor, in full)__,

4. The said minor (infant) on behalf of whom this application is being made, was born on the _____day of the month of _____19_____, in the city of _____, state of _____, and said minor is a citizen of _____by birth / naturalization,* and he/she has been such a citizen for at least six months prior to the submission of this application.
    ** Annexed hereto is the minor's birth certificate [OR, a certified transcript of his/her birth] showing his/her date and place of birth.

5. The said minor is _____years of age, and he/she is single and never has been married, and lives with the undersigned at this address : _____

6. Petitioner is related to the minor in the following manner: **[state information herein]**

7. The grounds and reasons for which this change is being sought are as follows:
    [Set forth here the reasons for which you want the name changed]

Example, (say, it has to do with the child's need to develop family bond and identity with a stepfather's family):
    Petitioner, the minor's mother herein, has been married to a second husband, namely,
Mr._____, since _____19_____, and has since assumed his surname, and the couple now

---

•   Strike out one or the other word or phrase that does not apply.
**   Cross out this statement, if the facts are not so.

Petition for (Minor's)

have two other children by this marriage. The minor child for which this petition is being filed has experienced confusion and embarrassment at home and at school on account of the fact that his surname differs from that of the rest of his current family. Hence, petitioner desires to change the minor's surname to **[the proposed name]**. *Petitioner is informed, and truly believes, that such a change will protect the child from continued confusion and embarrassment, make him more secure and self-assured, and give him a sense of oneness with his two half-siblings and the entire present family.*

OR

Petitioner desires to change the minor's surname, which is **?? (say, "GIVENS")** , *to the surname proposed herein, namely,* **?? (say, "DAVIDSON")** , *because the name of the minor's natural father is John Davidson. The Affidavit of the said John Davidson is herewith annexed confirming his fatherhood and consenting to the minor's change of name*
.

NOTE: Now, for Paragraphs 8, 9, 10 and 11 herein, petitioners should strike out any and all clauses that are not applicable and should not include same, taking care, instead, to substitute clauses more fitting to one's particular circumstances. Note that in situations when the necessary consent of both or one of the minor's parents is not forthcoming, then the customary procedure is for the petitioning party to add a clause in the petition setting forth the reason(s) why petition is without such written consent. [**A typical clause could be one or more of paragraphs 8 to 11 herein, as may be applicable to a given petitioner's circumstances.**]

8. Annexed hereto is the AFFIDAVIT OF CONSENT OF THE PARENT OR GUARDIAN OF THE MINOR, from Mr./Mrs._____, the other parent/guardian of the minor, in support of the proposed change of name.

OR

9. The other parent [OR, both parent, is applicable] of the minor, by name of Mr./Mrs._____, who formerly resided at _____, is/are deceased, having died on or about this date:_____ [Annexed hereto is the death certificate attesting to this.]

(enter information as necessary or applicable)

OR

10. Petitioner duly requested the minor's other parent, whose name is Mr./Mrs._____, to grant his written consent to the proposed change of name for the minor, but no such consent was forthcoming; thereupon, petitioner sent the said Mr./Mrs._____ _____, a NOTICE OF PETITION TO NON-CONSENTING PARENT, duly notifying him/her of the date, time and place at which this petition is to be presented for consideration before this court, and no further response has been had to date from the said non-consenting parent. [Annexed hereto is a true copy of the said Notice of Petition sent to him/her, and of the Receipt of Certified Mail by which the notice was sent.]

OR

11. Petitioner prays the court to dispense altogether with service of a notice of this petition upon Mr./Mrs. _____, the other parent (guardian) of the minor herein, for the reason that petitioner has exhausted all due diligence and all avenues in attempting to locate the said person, but to no avail, the following being some of the major attempts made: *[List the persons and sources contacted, by what means made, the dates made and the results gotten on each, etc.]*

Petition (Minor's)   **Copyright © 1990, 1997**
                                                DO-IT-YOURSELF LEGAL PUBLISHERS, Newark, N.J.

12.   The minor, the object of this petition, has never been convicted of any crimes.

13.   There are no debts, judgments or liens, and no court actions or proceedings currently outstanding to which the minor is a party; the minor has never been adjudicated a bankrupt, and there are no claims, demands, liabilities, or obligations on a written instrument or otherwise which are currently outstanding against the minor. *[If the facts happen to be otherwise, however, then just set forth the essential details herein—such debts, judgments, liens, court actions or claims or liabilities as are involved, to whom owed and for what, etc.]*

14.   The minor is employed as follows: he/she is a student in grade_____ at the following school: *[enter details, as may be applicable].*

15.   * A published or written notice of intention to make this application was published [OR, was served upon Mr./Mrs. _____ of this address:_____ by Certified Mail on _____(date)_____] in the following newspaper:_____ _____ in the issue of _____(date)_____; and a true copy of the Notice, as published [OR, as served], is attached herewith as well as the AFFIDAVIT OF PUBLICATION (OR, AFFIDAVIT OF SERVICE).

16.   No person will be adversely affected or prejudiced in anyway by the proposed change of name herein.

17.   No application for an order of name change concerning the minor child herein has previously been made by petitioner.

**WHEREFORE, petitioner prays the court to grant this application, authorizing the minor, the object of the within application, to assume the proposed name, namely: *[the proposed name of the minor, in full]*, inasmuch as the proposed change of name would be beneficial to the minor, and to his/her best interests and welfare, and is not intended for any fraudulent or wrongful purpose, or to interfere with the legitimate rights of others in any way.

Signed (name, in full): 1._____ **(sign here, in full)**
                                                                    (Petitioner) ↗

(Date on which you
signed and notarized this)   2._____
                                          (The Minor—if over 14 years of age) ↗
Dated, this _____   **(His/her original name, in full)**
day of _____ 19____

---

* NOTE: If your state's procedures either uses an Order-to-Show-Cause method, or requires the serving of a Notice-of-Intention-to-File on certain parties in advance of the actual filing, you will probably have to include a clause such as this in your petition. If the circumstances are otherwise, it probably won't be necessary and should be excluded or deleted.
** *Use this clause, instead, when your state's procedures employ an order-to-show-cause method:*
        [WHEREFORE, petitioner prays the court to sign an Order-to-Show-Cause designating a specified time and place wherein cause is to be shown why this application for change of name should not be granted; and, that upon hearing, that the court make an order authorizing the minor herein to assume the proposed name, which is: **[name Proposed, in full]**, inasmuch as the proposed change of name would be the best interests and welfare of the minor and is not intended for any fraudulent or wrongful purpose, or to interface with the legitimate rights of others in any way.

54

Individual Verification
to Petition

Index No. __(enter this)__

STATE OF_____,
COUNTY OF_____SS.:

(Petitioners' present name, in full)

I/We _____↓_____, being duly sworn, say: I am (we are)

the _____**PETITIONER**_____in the within case or matter; I (we) have read the

foregoing/annexed document, ___**FILLED PETITION FOR A CHANGE OF NAME**___,

and know the contents thereof; the same is true of my (our) own knowledge, except as to

the matters therein stated to be alleged on information and belief, and as to those matters I

(we) believe them to be true.

Sworn to before me on the _____

day of _____ 19 _____.

SIGNED: __*(Petitioner sign present, full name)*__

The name signed must be printed herewith

SIGNED: __*(Second Petitioner, if any, signs)*__

name signed must be printed beneath

_____

(Notary Public)

My commission Expires:

_____19_____.

Order, Minor—New York

(Leave blank)

At a Special Term Part_____

_____ of the (name of the court)

of the City/State of_____,

(Enter those for where court is located) _____ held in and for the county of

_____,at the county's

courthouse thereof, on the _____

day of _____ 19 _____.

(Leave blank for court clerk)

PRESENT:

Hon.

(Get Judge's name from the clerk)
Justice/Judge

Re: **Application of** *(adult petitioner's name, in full)*

To Change the Name of *(minor's present name, in full)* _____ **an infant,**

To: *(minor's proposed name, in full)*

Enter These

ORDER/DECREE GRANTING CHANGE OF NAME (Minor's)

Index No. (Enter this)

Upon reading the Verified Petition filed by *[petitioner's name , in full]* _____,
for and on behalf of *[the minor's present name, in full]* _____, an infant,
and presented this day before me, requesting leave of this Court for the said infant to
assume another name, viz: *[proposed name for the minor, in full]* _____ in
place of his/her present name; and upon reviewing the supporting Affidavits(s), birth
certificate and/or other evidence presented herewith in proof and support of the
petitioner's application thereof; and it appearing that the allegations in the Verified
Petition are true, and that the infant subject of this petition is a citizen of _____
_____, by birth/naturalization, and was born in the city of _____,

(Enter these details) County of _____, State of _____, on the _____ day of
_____ _____, 19 _____ bearing Birth Certificate No. *(enter it here, if known)*;
and it further appearing that the requirements for service of Notice of the proposed change
of name on non-petitioning parents or guardians herein have been met; that all parental
consents and/or notifications as are necessary have been obtained; and that the proposed
change of name is not for any fraudulent or wrongful purpose, and further, that the best
interests of the infant child herein will be substantially promoted by the proposed change,

NOW WHEREFORE, after due deliberations on the application herein, it is

ORDERED, that *(minor's present name, in full)* _____ the infant subject
of this petition, is authorized to assume the proposed name as *(his/her proposed name, in full)* _____ in place and stead of the present name, effective from the _____
day of _____ 19_____, upon the petitioner complying with the provisions
of this order, as follows:

(Clerk fills these in)

First, that this Order and the petition and all supporting papers upon which this
order is granted, be entered in the Office of the Clerk of this court within <u>10</u> days from the
date hereof; and second, that within <u>20</u> days from the date of entry of this order, a

(Minor's Order)

Notice of this order be published once in this newspaper: **(court fills this in**, the said notice to read substantially as follows:

(Newspaper in which notice is
to be published)

(Piece to be sent to newspaper for publication)

NOTICE is hereby given that an order entered by the *(name of the Court)* Court, *(enter)* County, on the_____ day of _____ 19____, bearing the Index Number *(enter #)* , a copy of which may be examined at the office of the clerk, located at *(address of court where petition is filed)* in Room *(get this from the clerk)* grant me the right, effective from the _____ day of _____ 19_____, to assume the name of *(proposed new name, in full)*_____. My present address is *(enter detail)*_____ _____; the date of my birth is *(enter)*_____at *(city and state)*; my present name is *(set forth, in full).*

and third, that thereafter, within <u>40</u> days from the date of this order, proof of the said publication shall, by affidavit, be filed and recorded in the office of the clerk of this court; and

that thereafter, namely, after the foregoing directives are complied with, the infant herein shall be known as *(the proposal name, in full*_____on and from the above specified effective date, and by no other name.*

ENTER:

(Leave blank, Judge signs

_____
JUDGE

---

* NOTE:

If the minor is either an Alien, or an ex-convict (see explanation pp. 31-32), then you may have to provide herein an additional paragraph to that effect, as follows:

Clause for Alien

and it is further ORDERED, that a copy of this Order be served by Certified Mail, upon the U.S. Immigration and Naturalization Service at *(address)*, within 10 days of the entry of this order, and that proof of such service be filed with the clerk of the court herein within 10 days thereafter.

Clause for prior criminal conviction

and it is further ORDERED, that a copy of this Order be served upon the Head, Division of Criminal Justice Service of this state, at *(address)*, within 10 days of the entry of this order, and that proof of such service be filed with the clerk of the court herein within 10 days thereafter.

(Parent's/Guardian's Consent)

Index No. **(Enter this # from the Court Clerk)**
_____

STATE OF_____,
COUNTY OF_____SS.:

AFFIDAVIT OF CONSENT OF MINOR'S PARENT OR GUARDIAN

I, the undersigned person, being duly sworn, respectfully declare and say:

That I am over 18 years of age, and reside at this address:_____

(enter these particulars for the minor) _____. That I am the natural father/mother* of the minor, whose birth name is: **(minor's present name, in full)**_____who was born on the _____ day of _____19_____, in the city/town of _____, County of _____, State of _____.

That a PETITION to change the name of the said child is being filed in court by the other natural parent of the minor, the object being to change the minor's name from the present name, as given above, to another name, namely: **(the minor's proposed names, in full)**_____.

I have fully read the said petition, and I hereby give my consent voluntarily to the proposed change of name for the minor, and assert no objection whatsoever to the petitioner's application thereof.

(The consenting party signs here)

Signed: _____ **(PARENT)**

Print Name signed, in full:_____

(Notary completes this .) Before me, a duly qualified Notary Public of the State of _____, County of _____ appeared Mr./Mrs. _____, to me known or made known to me to be the individual described in the within instrument, and who signed, acknowledged and sworn to the said instrument as true, on this _____ day of _____ 19 _____.

_____
(Notary Public's Seal)

* NOTE: Always enter the present or proposed names in full.

58

Index No. __(enter this)_____

AFFIDAVIT OF MINOR'S CONSENT IN SUPPORT OF PETITION TO CHANGE MINOR'S NAME

STATE OF_____,
COUNTY OF_____**SS.:**

I, the undersigned, being duly sworn, respectfully depose and say:

That I am under 18 (eighteen), but over 14 (fourteen) years of age.

(Enter these details of the minor) That my legal name at birth is **(enter same, in full)**_____, and I was born on the _____ day of _____ 19 _____, in the city/town of _____ County and State of _____.

That I am the object and beneficiary of a certain PETITION FOR A CHANGE OF NAME being filed with this court for me and on my behalf, to change my name from the present name, as aforementioned above, to **(enter new proposed name, in full)** .

That I have read the contents of the said petition; and I hereby aver that I agree with same, and give my consent wholly and voluntarily to the proposed change of name and the petition thereof.

WHEREFORE, I respectfully pray the court to approve the proposed change of my name pursuant to the said petition herein.

(Minor signs present names, in full)
↓
Signed: _____ **(MINOR CHILD)**

Print Name signed, in full:_____

(To be filled in by the Notary Public) Before me, a duly qualified Notary Public of the State of _____, County of _____ appeared Mr./Mrs. _____ to me known or made known to me to be the individual described in the within instrument, and who signed, acknowledged and sworn to the said instrument as true, on this _____ day of _____ 19 _____.

_____
(Notary Public's Seal)

(Notice To Non-Consenting Parent/Spouse)

The _____ Court of the State/City of _____,
County of _____.

Index No. __(enter this)__

Re: In the Matter of the Application by
(adult pet's name, in full) to change the
name of _(minor's present name, in full)_,
a minor/adult, to this Name: _(new name,_
in full) _____

NOTICE OF PETITION TO NON-CONSENTING PARENT (OR SPOUSE)

TO: Mr./Mrs./Ms. _(enter full name of the party to be noticed)_
Address: _(his/her mailing address)_ _____

Sir: PLEASE TAKE NOTICE that an application (petition) requesting an Order of the court to change the name of a minor, _(enter minor's present name in full)_, to another name, namely, _(proposed new name, in full)_ _____, a true copy of which is attached herewith, has been filed with, and will be presented for consideration or hearing to the above captioned court at this address: _(the court clerk's office)_ _____, Room_____, on this date _(confirm this with clerk)_, at 9:30 a.m. thereof.

You are hereby invited to file in writing, any objections, if any, to the granting of the petition with the Clerk of the Court and with the undersigned, on or before this date: _(get this date from the clerk)_ , and to further appear at the above stated hearing date and place for a hearing, and in case of your failure to answer or to appear, an Order may be entered by default for the relief sought in this notice, as set forth above.

Dated: _(date on which sent)_
County and State:_____

Signed_____

Petitioner's name (printed)_____

Your Return Address:_____

_____

(Affidavit Of Service)

Index No. **(enter this)**

Re: In the Matter of the Application by **(petitioner's name, in full)**, to Change the Name of **(minor's name, in full)**, a minor/adult, to this Name: **(proposed new name, in full)**

AFFIDAVIT OF SERVICE OF NOTIFICATION TO AUTHORITIES NOTICE

State of _____
County of _____ ss.:

(Date when the papers were deposited in the mail depository)

Mr./Mrs./Ms. **(Petitioner's old name, in full)** _____, being duly sworn deposes and says: that he/she is the adult petitioner herein; that on the _____ day of _____ 19____, he served the within document(s), namely **(specify which documents)** _____, upon this person/authority **(enter name of the party served)** _____, by mailing, by Certified Mail, a true copy of the said document(s) securely enclosed in a post-paid wrapper in the Post-Office—a Branch Post-Office—regularly maintained by the United States Government. The said mail was addressed to the said person/authority as follows: **(set forth the address)** _____

(Address to which sent or addressed)

_____, which is the address previously designated by the party for that purpose, or the last known residence or place where said party then kept an office, between which places there then was and now is a regular communication by mail.

Signed: _____
(Adult Petitioner)

Sworn to before me, on this _____
day of _____ 19 _____

_____
(Notary Public)

CHAPTER  6

HOW TO FILE FOR CHANGE OF NAME IN YOUR STATE, IN ANY STATE IN THE UNION

A. Broad Similarities in Rules and Procedures Among States.

As has been repeatedly stressed and pointed out in several preceding sections of this manual (see, especially, Chap.3 at pp. 18-19, and Section A of Chapter 4, at p. 23), the good fortune for the readers of this manual is that the procedures, and, more particularly, the broad principles, involved in the undertaking of judicial change of name are by and large identical from one state to the other, with any differences usually relating merely to the state-specific particulars that are inevitably unique to each state—matters like the specific address, name or location of the appropriate court in which to file, the specific amount charged for filing, the particular newspaper in which to publish, and the like.

It is in light of this reality that the point was equally stressed in those earlier sections of this manual (see, especially Chapter 3 at pp. 18-19, and Section A of Chapter 4, at p. 23), that *if one is able to do a judicial name change—or merely able to follow the process of doing so—in the state of New York, then one can just as easily do one's legal name change in just about any other state of one's residence using the same basic knowledge outlined in the New York oriented Chapters 4 and 5 of the manual.* This is more especially so, it was pointed out, because of New York's special status as a premier pioneering state in the field of name change laws, because its age-old written laws, court decisions, and legal opinions on the matter have come to be widely copied across most states as the standard practice representing what is best on the subject matter.

With the foregoing in mind as a background, we outline below in this chapter, for the benefit of those who either live or want to change their names in **states other than New York,** the bare essentials for undertaking a legal change of name in the average state. Additionally, to further augment the information given in this chapter, a necessarily limited but essential summary of information for judicial name change in each of the 50 states, is provided in Appendix B, pp. 67-80. And don't forget the information of more generalized type contained in Chapter 3, "Some General Rules and Procedures Common to Name Change Petitions Everywhere". (pp. 18-22)

As you go through the contents set forth below, notice how very similar these rules and procedures tend to be to those of the state of New York's outlined in Chapters 4 and 5.

B. Step-by Step Procedures for Filing a Petition

BELOW IS AN OUTLINE OF THE GENERAL REQUIREMENTS AND PROCEDURES FOR LEGALLY CHANGING ONE'S NAME. YOU SHOULD UNDERTAKE YOUR NAME

CHANGING IN THE SAME **EXACT**, ORDERLY, STEP-BY-STEP SEQUENCE IN WHICH THE PROCEDURES ARE LISTED HERE:

Step 1 : FAMILIARIZE YOURSELF WITH THE BASIC BACKGROUND INFORMATION

Read chapters 1 and 3 (pp. 1-22), with particular attention paid to those sections of the chapters dealing with the minimum prerequisites and conditions for securing a court's approval of a petition, and the reasons and motives considered proper by the courts for changing one's name. See, also, Appendix B at pp. 67-80 for summary information on judicial change of name proceedings in each of the 50 states. For each state in Appendix B, a list of the appropriate kinds of forms required for filing for a name change is specified to facilitate ordering the forms or otherwise obtaining or preparing them.

Step 2 : OBTAIN THE NECESSARY FILING FORMS

How do you get a supply of the forms? You may, at times, be able to get a supply of the proper forms from a local commercial or legal stationery store. As a practical matter, however, most would often carry only a limited or inappropriate variety of such forms, and others will have none at all. Hence, for the added convenience of our readers, Do-It-Yourself Legal Publishers makes available to its readership a **standard** or state-prescribed set of forms that will suffice for most filings. And for those few number of states for which the state-prescribed forms are not available, we provide, nevertheless, all-in-one package of forms; these all-in-one forms fully incorporate sufficient details as to meet most states' filing needs and requirements. And, even in some rare instances when the forms may not be wholly adequate for a particular state's requirements, they need only be adapted by the user to his special needs, with some minor modifications. [Samples of state-specific forms for a few select states are reproduced in Appendix D]

To order the Publisher's package of forms, just complete the "Order Form" on p. 111 and send it away to the Publisher's address given therein. Simply ask for the "Name Change Package of Forms", and specify the following: (i) whether you want the forms for an "adult" person or for a "minor"; (ii) in what specific state and locality you plan to file.

Step 3 : FILL OUT THE PETITION FORMS

Listed below are the illustrative samples of the forms you shall have obtained. To complete your forms, fill them out in the same way and in the **EXACT** order in which the forms are listed:

NOTE: In completing any forms whatsoever, always use the <u>full</u> names on all papers (for existing, as well as for the proposed names); sign all papers in <u>full</u> names, and be consistent all through - same spellings, and so on. Write the names in normal order - the last names go last.

1. Petition for Change of Name, With The Individual Verification Form [Sample illustrated preparation of this form is on p. 35 for an adult's, and   p. 51 for a minor's petition.]

2. Notice of (Filing) Petition·[Sample illustrated preparation of form is on p. 88 for both and adult's and a minor's petition]

3. Notice of Hearing on the Application for Name Change - applicable in certain states, usually instead of the Notice of Petition. (See a sample copy on pp. 88 or 103)

4. Affidavit of Service of Notification to Authorities—need for this mostly arises in petitions involving an alien, an attorney, or an ex-convict. [Sample illustrated preparation of this form is on p. 43, and the process for signing, notarizing, and filing away this affidavit with the court, is outlined under "STEP 7" of Chapter 4, on pp. 27 & 33]

5. Decree (Order) Granting Change of Name·[Sample illustrated preparation of this form is on p. 40 for an adult's petition, and on p. 55 for a minor's]

PUBLISHER'S NOTE: A 'national' version of the DECREE/ORDER form, considered in our estimation to be more suitable to the requirements of the vast majority of all states, will generally be provided to non-New York readers who order our all-state forms. (See p. 106 of the manual for the adult's version of this form.)

FORMS THAT APPLY ONLY IN MINOR'S NAME CHANGE SITUATION

6a. Consent Affidavit of the Wife/Husband—applicable only in adult's petitions, usually when the name being changed is the family name (surname). [Sample illustrated preparation of form is on p. 42]

6b. Affidavit of Consent by Minor's Parent/Guardian in Support of Petition - applicable only in minor's petitions, where the other parent is in support, willing to give his/her consent. [Sample illustrated preparation of form is on p. 57]

7. Affidavit of Minor's Consent in Support of Petition - applicable only in minor's petitions, and where the minor "joins" in the petition because he/she is within a certain higher age bracket, say, 14 or older. [Sample illustrated preparation of form is on p. 58]

8. Notice of Petition to Non-Consenting Parent (or Spouse) in Minor's (Spouse's) Name Change - need for this mostly arises in petitions involving **minors**, where the other party refuses to consent but his/her <u>address</u> <u>and</u> <u>whereabouts</u> <u>is</u> <u>at</u> <u>least</u> <u>known</u> to petitioner. [Sample illustrated preparation of this form is on p. 59; and the procedures for giving the actual notification to a non-consenting parent (or a spouse) are outlined under "STEP 5" of Chapter 5, on p. 49]

Step 4 : SIGN AND NOTARIZE THE PAPERS, AS APPROPRIATE

[See "STEP 4" on pp. 26-7, and "STEP 4" on p. 48, for general pointers and procedures on which papers are to be signed and **notarized** and how, for adult-type and minor-type petitions, respectively]

In brief, generally sign (and/or <u>notarize</u>) the papers at the spots marked "X".

Step 5 : FILE THE PAPERS WITH THE COURT

[See "STEP 5" on pp. 27-8, for an adult's petition, and "STEP 5" on pp. 49, for a minor's, for pointers and procedures for properly putting your papers together and finally filing them with the court clerk's office]

NOTE: If a state using "show-cause-order" procedure, such as California, you'll follow a slightly different procedure at this juncture: rather than file all the petition papers and then await for either the judge's signature approving the application, or the setting of a hearing, you will, instead, do the following: (i) submit ("file") the "Petition for Change of Name" and the "Order to Show Cause" papers with the court clerk as a start; then (ii) upon the Order to Show Cause being signed by the court, you'll either have the Order published in a designated newspaper, or have it properly delivered ("served") to some designated "interested parties"; (iii) it will then be time to go to court for a hearing ("STEP 6" below), at which occasion it would probably be time for you to submit to court the rest of your petition papers—Proof of Publication from the newspaper, Final Decree Granting Change of Name, any papers of objections received from an opposing spouse or parent, if any, and the like; and, (iv) finally, upon the court approving the name change application, the judge would sign the (final) Decree Granting Change of Name to conclude the matter.

Step 6 : ATTEND THE COURT HEARING, IF THERE'S ONE

[See "STEP 6" on pp. 28-32, for general pointers on hearings for name change petitions. Where the object of the petition is a minor person, you may further see "STEP 6" on p. 49, for some additional details]

Step 7 : PUBLISH A NOTICE OF THE PETITION OR OF THE NAME CHANGE (OR "POST" ON DESIGNATED PUBLIC PLACE)

[See "STEP 7" of Chapter 4 on pp. 32-3 for general pointers on the concluding procedures following either a hearing on the petition, on the one hand, or an outright approval of the petition without a hearing, on the other hand. Where the object of the petition is a minor, you may further refer to "STEP 7" of Chapter 5 for some additional information]

An important part of the name change process common to the overwhelming majority of states, is the giving of some formal public "notice" of the change—by publication, for most states. Not all states, though, require the giving of such notice; there are some states, far fewer in number, that do not require it. The timing or frequency of the notice, as well as the actual format of such notice, also differ from state to state.

Depending on the procedures followed by your particular state of filing (refer to Appendix B, pp. 67-80), you may have to give such notice, if any, BEFORE the hearing and the final signing by the judge of the final Order of Name change approving the change; or, alternatively, you may have to do so AFTER such hearing or the signing of the final Order of Name Change approval by the judge. Certain states—only a handful—even require that the notice be given before the filing of the petition is done.

By and large, such notice is generally given by having a written statement ("NOTICE") of the filing of the petition, or of the name change, published in appropriate newspaper, one usually published or widely read and circulated in the county wherein the petition is filed. (Some states, very few in number, merely require a "posting" of the notice in a designated public place, such as the public announcement board of the courthouse.)

How do you actually do the publication (or posting) - i.e., give the NOTICE? The actual process itself is simple. For the most part, after you shall have filed the name change petition with the court clerk, the clerk will inform you (especially if you politely request him to!) as to whether some publication (or posting) of a formal notice s required under your state's or county's procedures, or whether no notice at all is necessary. Combining the information you can get from Appendix B (pp. 67-80) of the manual, with the information you can get from your court clerk, you should be well informed on such matters as the timing and frequency of the publication that is to be made, the names of the newspapers that are acceptable to the local court for making the publication, and whether the notice is required to be published before <u>or</u> after the hearing on your petition (if any is applicable), or before <u>or</u> after the final order is signed by the judge, and so on. (TIP: Whenever in doubt, call up or visit your court clerk and ask!)

Thereafter, here's what you do: contact (and do this <u>promptly</u>!) the newspaper or newspapers recommended by your Name Change Clerk (or designated by the Order of the court, if more applicable), and get from them the price quote on what is their charge for having the Notice published for you. Then, send the newspaper a copy of the NOTICE piece, plus a check to cover the charge for the publication. And <u>do</u> <u>this</u> <u>promptly</u>, <u>without</u> <u>delay</u> at all. Now, upon the newspaper completing the publication of the Notice, the paper will send you a document called, **"AFFIDAVIT OF PUBLICATION".** This document is, simply, a notarized (i.e., sworn) statement signed by the newspaper's publisher by which the publisher certifies that his paper has, in fact, carried out the required publication of the notice. (See a sample copy of this affidavit reproduced on p. 44).

Now, all you do is take this document, the **AFFIDAVIT OF PUBLICATION,** and have it filed and recorded with the name change court clerk as proof to the court that you did fulfil the "notice" requirement.
(SEE SAMPLES OF TWO DIFFERENT FORMATS OF A "NOTICE" ON PP. 88 & 97)

 **Step** : NOW, GET YOUR NEW NAME RECOGNIZED IN "OFFICIAL" CIRCLES

[See the procedures outlined in "STEP 8" of Chapter 4, p. 33 above, and follow those same procedures herein]

APPENDIX **A**

LIST OF SAMPLE FORMS CITED IN THIS MANUAL
(Where to Find Them)

APPENDIX B

SUMMARY OF BASIC LAWS AND RULES
FOR CHANGE OF NAME IN ALL 50 STATES

This appendix summarizes the state-specific essentials of the laws, rules and procedures for legal name change in each of the 50 states and the District of Columbia. The information incorporates changes and amendments governing judicial change of name contained in the statute books as of 1997. *Of course, laws and court rules do change (and may change) at any time. So, in any event, you may still want to check your state's latest name change code, or to simply ask your local name change court clerk before proceeding.*

The information in this appendix comes, for the most part, from each state's legal codes, those parts of your state statutes that contain name change laws. The citations for the specific state laws governing the change of names, are given under the caption "STATUTES".

This appendix, read and used in conjunction with the relevant sections of the manual (Chapters 3 & 6, particularly), will ensure that almost any American wanting to undertake his or her own legal name change shall have had in his/her hands the basic essentials to do so in almost any state in the United States.

ALABAMA: "Declaration" for change of name is filed in the Probate Court setting forth the reasons for which the change is sought.
Basic Form required for filing: Declaration (Petition) For Name Change; Order/Decree Granting Change of Name.
STATUTE: Ala. Code t. 13,§278 (1958)

ALASKA: Petition is filed in the Superior Court. Change of Name will generally be granted if "the court finds sufficient reasons for the change and also finds it consistent with the public interest".
Basic Form required for filing: Verified Petition; Order/Decree Granting Change of Name
STATUTE: Alaska Stat. §09.55.010 (1962)

ARIZONA: Application is filed in the Superior Court of the petitioner's county of residence setting forth the reasons for which the change is sought. Minor child over 16 years of age may file his/her own application. Upon filing the application, the court may, if it deems it necessary in a given instance, order petitioner to give notice of the application by publication or by service of notice, on any party the court may designate.
Basic Form required for filing: Verified Petition; Notice of Hearing; Order Granting Change of Name
STATUTE: Ariz. Rev. StatAnn.§12-601,12-602 (1956)

ARKANSAS: Application is filed in the Chancery or Circuit Court setting forth "good reasons" for which the change is sought. Thereafter, applicant shall be known, and shall sue and be sued, by the new name.
Basic Form required for filing: Application (Petition); Order Granting Change of Name
STATUTE: Ark Stat. Ann.§34-801 to 34-803 (1947), §82-507 (1960)

68

CALIFORNIA: Petition is made to the Superior Court of your county of residence setting forth the reasons for which the name change is sought, with notice of the proposed change given by an "Order to Show Cause"* format, by direct service or by publication, to any parties in interest. A hearing is conducted and the judge signs the order granting the proposed change. For a minor under the age of 18, the petition is made on the minor's behalf by the parent, guardian, relative or next friend.

California is somewhat unique in name changing methods in that it uses a "Show-cause-order" procedure. Thus, contrary to the New York type "direct petition" format more commonly employed in most states wherein a petitioner would merely file his application with the court and presuppose no advance third party opposition to the undertaking, the state of California employs a slightly different format which, in effect, presupposes that there are some potential objecting parties who, therefore, need to be alerted to the filing right at the onset. Under the format employed by this latter group of states, here's the procedure: (i) petitioner will first prepare a preliminary order - the ORDER TO SHOW CAUSE; (ii) petitioner then takes the Order to court (along with the "Petition for Change of Name"), and gets the clerk to enter within the Order a set date for a hearing on the application and to have the judge sign it; (iii) upon being signed, the petitioner will pick up a copy of the signed Order to Show Cause (a document which primarily orders anyone who may have any objection to the petition to come to court on a specified hearing date and there to "Show Cause" why such an objection should be heeded) and then get it either published in a designated local newspaper, or properly "served" on (delivery to) some designated persons named in the Order; (iv) petitioner then proceeds to keep the hearing date, following which the judge will either grant the name change application, or deny it accordingly. If granted, the judge will sign the Decree Granting Change of Name, and it's done!
Basic Form required for filing: Order To Show Cause; Verified Petition; Order Granting Change of Name
STATUTES: Cal. Civ. Pro. §1275-1279 (West 1972), Cal. Civ. §1096 (West 1955) (deeds), Cal. Corp. §3600 (West 1964). Cal. Elections §214 (West), Cal. Health and Safety §10460-10462 (West Supp. 1972) (amendment of birth records, naturalization)

COLORADO: Petition is filed in the District or County court of the petitioner's county of residence setting forth the reasons for seeking the change. The court will generally sign the order granting the name change, if the court is satisfied that it is proper and not detrimental to any person. Notice of the said change of name is to be published at least 3 times within 20 days from the date of the signing of the court order, such publication being made in a newspaper named in the Order by the court that is published in petitioner's county of residence.
Basic Form required for filing: Verified Petition; Order Granting Change of Name; Notice of Name Change.

STATUTE: Colo. Rev. Stat. Vol. 6A, Art. 15, 13-15-101.

CONNETICUT: Petition is filed in the Probate Court (and, in a few counties, the Superior Court) that is located in the petitioner's county of residence. Upon such filing, the court notifies the parties of the date set for hearing, if any is to be had. A person owning or having an interest in real estate whose name is changed, must, within 20 days after such change, file a certificate, duly acknowledged, giving old and new names.
Basic Form required for filing: Application (Petition); Order Granting Change of Name.
STATUTES: Conn. Gen. Stat. Ann. §52-11 (1958), §45-69 (1958) (adoption), §47-12 (1958), §47-12a (1973 Supp.) (real estate)

DELAWARE: Petition is filed in the Superior Court of the county of residence . The petition must first be published in a newspaper published in the county in which petition is to be filed, for at least once a week for 3 weeks before the petition is filed. The court may grant the petition if there appears no reason for not granting it. A minor over the age of 14 must also sign the petition for the change of the minor's name.
Basic Form required for filing: Verified Petition; Order Granting Change of Name.
STATUTE: Del. Code Ann. Tit. 10, §5901-5905 (1953), 13, §1536 (1953) (divorce)

DISTRICT OF COLUMBIA Application is filed by a resident of the District in the District Court of the District. Notice of the filing of the application is published once a week in "a newspaper in general circulation published in the District" for 3 consecutive weeks prior to the hearing being had. Petition for a minor is filed by the parent, guardian or next friend.
Basic Form required for filing: Application (Petition); Notice of Filing; Order Granting Change of Name.
STATUTE: D.C. Code Ann. §16-2501-2503, (1966), §16-312 (1966) (adoption)

FLORIDA: Petition is filed in the Chancery Court (and, in a few counties, in the Circuit Court) of the petitioner's county of residence, showing the reasons for wanting the change. A hearing on the petition may be had promptly after the filing of the petition, and the court may thereafter sign a final judgment decreeing the change. For a minor's petition, the other parent must grant a written consent, otherwise such parent (the non-consenting party) is to be properly served with notice of the proposed change. A non-consenting parent residing in another state may be served by publication.
Basic Form required for filing: Verified Petition; Final Judgment of Name Change.
STATUTE: West Fla. Stat. Ann. Vol. 5, 68.07. Fla. Stat. Ann. Const. Art. 3, §11 (1969), §62,031 (1969), §104-24 (1960) (elections), §97,103 (1972 Supp.) (registration), §322.19 (1968) (license)

GEORGIA: Petition and Notice of filing petition are filed in the Superior Court of the petitioner's county of residence. Within 7 days of such filing, the notice of filing is to be published in "the official legal organ of the county" named by the court, once a week for 4 weeks to enable objections, if any, to be filed. The court may authorize the change, so long as the intent is not fraudulent or designed to deprive another of his or her legal rights.

Basic Form required for filing: Verified Petition; Notice of Filing; Order Granting Name Change.

STATUTE: Official Code of GA. Ann. Vol. 16, Tit. 19, 19-12-1 - 19-12-3

HAWAII: Petition may be filed with either the lieutenant governor's office or with the Family Court. Notice of change of name signed by the lieutenant governor shall be published in the state once, in a newspaper of general circulation designated in the order for change.

Basic Form required for filing: Verified Petition; Notice of Name Change; Order Granting Name Change.

STATUTE: Hawaii Rev. Stat §574-1 to §574-5 (1968)

IDAHO: Application is made to the District court covering the area where the applicant resides. Notice of hearing on the application is published for 4 successive weeks. A petition by a male under 21 years of age, or a female under 18 years, is filed by the parent, guardian, near relative or friend.

Basic Form required for filing: Application (Petition); Notice of Hearing on the Application; Order Granting Name Change.

STATUTE: Idaho Code §7-801 (1948), §7-802 to 804 (1972 Supp.)

ILLINOIS: Petition is made to the Circuit Court, Chancery Division thereof, of the petitioner's county of residence. For adult applications, a notice of the petition is published in a newspaper designated by the court for three consecutive weeks, the first publication to be done at least 6 weeks before the petition is filed. (In Chicago, the publication is made in the Chicago Law Bulletin.) A hearing may thereafter be held on the application. If no reason appears why the request should be denied, it will be granted by the court.

Basic Form required for filing: Verified Petition; Notice of Petition; Judgment (Order) of Name Change.

STATUTE: I LL. Ann. Stat. Ch. 96, §1-10 (Smith-Hurd 1971), 46, §6-54 (Smith-Hurd 1966) (elections)

INDIANA: Petition is filed in the Circuit Court of the petitioner's county of residence. Notice of filing petition must be published consecutively (i.e., one after the other) by three different weekly publications, the last of which must be at least 30 days before the hearing. Hearing is held thereafter on the petition before the judge may sign an order approving the change.

Basic Form required for filing: Verified Petition; Notice of Filing;

Order Granting Change of Name.
STATUTE: Ind. Ann. Stat. §3-801 to §3-805 (1968, 1972 Supp.), §29-3428 (1969) (elections)

IOWA: Petition is filed with the clerk of the District Court setting forth reasons for which the change is desired, and listing the estate owned, if any. Petitioner must be a resident of the county where the petition is filed. No person may change name more than once under the statute.
Basic Form required for filing: Verified Petition; Order Granting Change of Name.
STATUTE: Iowa Code Ann. §674.1-674.14 (1973 Supp.)

KANSAS: Petition is filed in the District Court of the petitioner's county of residence, showing the reasons for the proposed change and that petitioner has been a resident of the state for at least 60 days. Public notice of hearing on the petition is to be given, either by mail or by publication, in the discretion of the court. If notice is directed to be given by publication, such publication is to be made in the appropriate newspaper for 3 consecutive weeks; and if the notice is directed to be given by mail, service of such notice is to be made by registered or certified mail to "parties in interest" named by the court. The hearing is held at least 30 days after the first publication, and the judge may order the name change if the judge is satisfied that "there is reasonable cause" for making the change.
Basic Form required for filing: Verified Petition; Notice of Hearing on the Petition; Order Granting Change of Name.
STATUTE: Kan. Stat. Ann. Vol. 4A, Art. 14 #60-1401

KENTUCKY: Adult petitioner (i.e., one over 18) may file a petition, or, if an infant, petition is made for him by the parent or guardian, and is filed in the District Court of the petitioner's county of residence. Notice of filing of petition shall be served on a non-consenting parent or guardian, if such party refuses or is unavailable to sign a statement of consent for proposed change of name for a minor child. With respect to a minor's petition, a hearing may be held to enable the court determine whether such change is "in the best interest" of the minor.
Basic Form required for filing: Verified Petition; Notice of Filing of Petition; Order Granting Change of Name.
STATUTE: Ky Rev. Stat. Ann. §401.010-§401.040 (1972), §117.735 (1971) (election)

LOUISIANA: Petition is filed in the District Court of the petitioner's parish of residence. Minor petition is filed by the parents, tutor or special tutor of the child. The District Attorney must then be served with a notice of the petition (or just a copy of the petition), and his "answer" or response submitted to the court. Following the hearing (if any is had), the Judge signs the Judgment approving the change.
Basic Form required for filing: Verified Petition; District Attorney's Proposed Answer to the Petition; Judgement (Order) of Name Change.

STATUTE: La. Rev. Stat. §13:4751-4755(1968)

MAINE: Petition is filed addressed to the Judge of Probate Court of the petitioner's county of residence. Petition for a minor is made by the legal guardian, but notice must be given to the other parent, or a written consent obtained from him or her.
Basic Form required for filing: Verified Petition; Notice of Petition (Minors); Order Granting Name Change.
STATUTE: Me. Rev. Stat. Ann. Tit. 19, §781 (1964).

MARYLAND: Petition is filed in the Circuit Court, Equity Division, of the petitioner's county of residence. Minor's petition is filed for him by the parent or the legal guardian. A notice of posting is ordered posted by the judge (Order to Post) and is then posted by the county sheriff for 30 days on the bulletin board of the courthouse. The judge may sign judgment approving the name change thereafter.
Basic Form required for filing: Verified Petition with a Motion for an Order to Post (or to Publish); Notice of Posting; Order for Posting; Judgement (Order) for Name Change.
STATUTE: Md. Ann. Code art. 16,§123 (1957), 9B Md. Ann. Code. Md. Rules BH 70-75 (1957)

MASSACHUSETTS: Petition is filed in the Probate Court of the petitioner's county of residence (attach birth certificate). Public notice of hearing on the petition is required to be given - by publication of the notice of hearing once in a court designated newspaper published in the locality. The judge signs the decree (order) thereafter approving the change.
Basic Form required for filing: Verified Petition; Request for Information (Adults only); Affidavit Disclosing Care or Custody Proceedings (minors only); Notice of Hearing; Decree Granting Name Change.
STATUTE: Mass. Ann. Laws ch.210, §12 (1958)

MICHIGAN: An adult person (over 18 years old) may file a petition in the Probate court; petitioner must have resided in the county for at least one year. Upon the filing of petition, the court shall set a time and place for hearing on the petition, and order publication of notice of change. Minor child over 16 years old who is to be a party to a proposed name change, must sign a written consent in the presence of the court before the court may approve an order changing the name of the minor child or include his name in the order to change. Petition to change the name of a minor under the age of 16, may not be approved, unless such minor is the natural or adopted child of the petitioner, and unless a jointly signed petition or the joint written consent of both parents is submitted, or from the surviving parent, if one parent is dead.
Basic Form required for filing: Verified Petition; Notice of Name Change: Order Granting Change of Name..
STATUTE: Mich. Stat. Ann. Vol. 20, Chap. X1,Sec. 27.3178 (561)(562)

MINNESOTA: The petitioner, who must have been resident in the county of filing for at least one year, files the petition in the District Court. The petition must describe lands in which the petitioner (and his children and spouse, if their names are also to be changed by the application) has any interest or liens, if any. Petitioner must appear personally before the court and prove his/her identity by at least two witnesses, and if a minor, his guardian must appear on his behalf. A minor's name may be changed only with both of his parents having notice of the pending of the application to change his name, to the extent practicable as determined by the court.
Basic Form required for filing: Application (Petition); Order Granting Change of Name..
STATUTE: Minn. Stat. Ann. §259.10, 259.11 (1971), §518.27 (1969) (divorce), §201.14 (1969) (elections)

MISSISSIPPI: Petition is filed in the Chancery Court of the petitioner's county of residence, setting forth the reasons why the change is sought.
Basic Form required for filing: Verified Petition; Order Granting Name Change.
STATUTE: Miss. Code Ann. §1269-01, 1269-02 (1943)

MISSOURI: Petition is made to the Circuit Court of the petitioner's county of residence. The judge will sign the order approving the name change, if the court satisfies itself that the change "would be proper and (not) detrimental to the interests of any other person". Upon approval, the judge will sign the order granting the change, and will designate in the order the newspaper picked in which a notice of the name change is to be published. The notice of change is to be published in the designated newspaper for three times within 20 days from the date the name change order was signed.
Basic Form required for filing: Verified Petition; Notice of Name Change; Order Granting Name Change.
STATUTE: Mo. Rev. Stat. §527.270-527.290 (1959)

MONTANA: Petition is filed in the District Court of the petitioner's county of residence. If the party is a minor (under 21 years of age), the petition is filed for him or her by the parent or guardian. Notice of hearing on the petition is to be published for 4 successive weeks; objections to the change, if any, may be filed by interested persons, and a hearing held thereafter by the court to made final determination on the granting of the petition.
Basic Form required for filing: Verified Petition; Notice of Hearing on the Petition; Order Granting Name Change.
STATUTE: Mont. Rev. Code Ann. §93-100-1 (1964) to §93-100-9 (1971) (1949, Supp. 1971)

NEBRASKA: Petition is filed in the District Court of the petitioner's county of residence; petitioner must be resident of the county of filing for at least one year. Notice of the filing of the petition must be published for 30

days in "some newspaper" of general circulation published in the county.
Basic Form required for filing: Verified Petition; Notice of Filing of Petition; Order Granting Name Change.
STATUTE: Neb. Rev. Stat. §61-101 to §61-104 (1971)

NEVADA: Petition (verified), addressed to the court, is filed with the District Court of the petitioner's district of residence. Notice of the filing of petition is to be published once a week for 3 successive weeks in "some newspaper of general circulation in the county". If within 10 days after the last publication of the notice there is no written objection filed with the court clerk by anyone, and good reason appears to have been shown for making the change, the court will sign the order granting the name change. And if objections are filed, a hearing is held and a final determination made thereafter by the court..
Basic Form required for filing: Verified Petition; Notice of Filing of Petition; Order Granting Name Change.
STATUTE: Nev. Rev. Stat. §41-270 to §41.290 (1971)

NEW HAMPSHIRE: Petition is filed with the Probate Court of the petitioner's county of residence. Petition will be granted if good cause is shown.
Basic Form required for filing: Verified Petition; Order Granting Name Change.
STATUTE: N.H. Rev. Stat. Ann. §547:7 (1955), §458:24 (1972 Supp.)

NEW JERSEY: Petition (complaint) is filed in the Superior Court of the petitioner's county of residence. The court, by order signed by the judge, sets a date for hearing on the petition and also designates therein the newspaper wherein notice of the application is to be published. Following the hearing, the judge will sign the Final Judgment approving the change. The Final Judgment signed by the judge will contain the "effective date" from when you are to begin to answer your new name and the name of a newspaper in which a copy of the Judgment is to be published. Hence, promptly upon the signing of the Final Judgment, you must immediately make a copy of same and send it to the newspaper designated in the Order so that it would have been published within 10 days of the "effective date". You must then file the original Judgment and the Proof (Affidavit) of publication of judgement (you'll get this back from the newspaper) with the county clerk's office, and file as well a "certified" copy of the Judgment with the Secretary of State's Office in Trenton NJ.

Basic Form required for filing: Verified Petition; Order Setting Date For Hearing; Final Judgment (Order) of Name Change; Notice of Application For Name Change.
STATUTE: N.J. Rev. Stat. §2A:52-1 to §2A:52-4 (1952, 1972-73 Supp). §2A:34-21 (1952)

NEW MEXICO: Petition is filed in the District Court of the petitioner's county of residence by a person who must be over 14 years of age. Notice of the making of the petition is published once per week for 2 consecutive weeks in a newspaper published in the county of filing. If there are no objections raised, and good reason appears to have been shown, the court will generally order the change; and if there are objections raised, a hearing is held and a final determination made thereafter.
Basic Form required for filing: Verified Petition; Notice of Petition; Order Granting Name Change.
STATUTE: N.M. Stat. Ann. §22-5-1 to §22-5-3 (1953)

NEW YORK: Petition is filed in the County Court or in the Supreme Court of the petitioner's county of residence. Or, if petitioner is a resident of the City of New York, such petitioner may file in either the Supreme Court or the Civil Court of the City of New York located in any county of the city. Infant's (minor's) petition is made by the parents, the next friend or guardian. If born within the state, the birth certificate (or a certificate that none is available) must be attached. Notice of the petition to change the name of a minor, must be served on the parents or guardians who are non-consenting to the proposed change, if any; such notice may, however, be dispensed with by the court if it is sufficiently shown that the person to be given notice cannot be located. Notice of the granting of the name change order must be published in a newspaper designated by the court and published in the county; the publication is to run for at least once within 20 days from the date of the signing of the order approving the change. The change takes effect not less than 30 days after the entry (signing) of the order approving the change. (see pp. 23-60 of the manual for fuller details of the law and procedures.)
Basic Form required for filing: Verified Petition; Order Granting Name Change (with Notice of Name Change as part thereof)
STATUTE: N.Y. Civ. Rights §60-63 (McKinney 1944, Supp. 1972)

NORTH CAROLINA: Application is filed with the clerk of the Superior court in the petitioner's county of residence setting forth "good reason" for the change and stating if name was ever changed before. Notice of the petition must be given by publication posted at the courthouse door for 10 days. Minor's application is made by the parent, guardian or next friend; abandonment of child by one parent vitiates the need for that parent's consent to changing of the child's name. For adult petitions (involving persons over the age of 16), the petitioning party must file proof of good character by two citizens, whereupon the order of name change is issued by the clerk. Only one change is permitted under the statute, but petitioner may assume former name, on making application to the court.
Basic Form required for filing: Verified Petition; Notice of filing Petition; Affidavit Testifying to Good Character (adult only); Order Granting Name Change

76

STATUTE: N. Car. Gen. Stat. §101-1 to §101-7 (1972), §20-676 (1965) (registration), §48-14 (1965) adoption).

NORTH DAKOTA: Petition is filed in the District Court of the petitioner's county of residence; petitioner must be a resident of the county of filing for at least 6 months before filing the petition. Notice of the application must, however, be published at least 30 days <u>prior to</u> the filing of the petition.
***Basic Form required for filing*:** Verified Petition; Notice of filing Petition; Order Granting Name Change
STATUTE: N. Dak. Cent. Code Ann. §32-28-01 to §32-28-04 (1960, Supp. 1971), §14-11-11 (1960) (adoption)

OHIO: Petition is filed in the Court of Common Pleas in the Probate Court Division thereof, of the petitioner's county of residence. Petitioner must be a bona fide resident of the county of filing for at least one year before the filing of the petition. Notice of the application must be published once in one newspaper of "general circulation" published in the county, at least (i.e., no earlier than) 30 days before the hearing date. A minor (under 18 years of age) must have the written consent of both living parents, or a hearing will be set on the matter, and the parent not consenting shall be given written notice of the hearing.
***Basic Form required for filing*:** Verified Petition; Notice of filing Petition; Order Granting Change of Name.
STATUTE: Ohio Rev. Code Ann. §2717.01 (Page 1954, Supp. 1972)

OKLAHOMA: Petition is filed in the District Court in the Civil Action Division thereof, by petitioner who shall have resided in the state for more than 30 days, and in the county of filing for more than 30 days immediately prior to the filing of the petition. A minor's petition is filed by the parent, guardian or next friend. Notice of filing of the petition is published once, for one week, at least 10 days prior to the date set for the hearing, and is to be published in "some newspaper authorized by law to publish legal notices" in the county wherein the petition is filed, or if no such newspaper is published in that county then in some newspaper of general circulation in the county which is printed in the state. The judicial method is exclusive; no change of name is permitted except as provided by the statute, or by marriage, decree of divorce, or adoption.
***Basic Form required for filing*:** Verified Petition; Notice of Petition; Judgment (Order) Granting Change of Name.
STATUTE: Okla. Stat. Ann. Tit. 12, §1631-1640 (1961)

OREGON: Depending on the county involved, the petition is filed in either the Domestic Relations Department or the Probate Department in the Circuit Court of the petitioner's county of residence, and must show "sufficient reasons" for the proposed change of name. A hearing is required on the petition. Public notice of the application must be given, first, by "posting" of a notice of the proposed change on the public

bulletin board of the courthouse <u>before</u> the hearing, and then, by posting of a notice of the decree granting the name change <u>after</u> the hearing. The birth certificates of the children will be changed upon the change of name by the parent.
Basic Form required for filing: Verified Petition; Notice of Hearing; Affidavit, Proof of Posting Notice; Decree of Change of Name; Notice of Change of Name.
STATUTE: Ore. Rev. Stat. §33.410 to §33.430 (1971)

PENNSYLVANIA: Petition is filed in the Court of Common Pleas of the petitioner's county of residence, setting forth the reasons for the proposed change and the petitioner's residences for the preceding 5 years, among other information. To win the court's approval, the contents of the application (the applicant's background) must show no judgments, liens or decrees of record against the petitioner. By an order made by the court, a notice of the filing of the petition and of the date set for the hearing thereof, is to be published in <u>two</u> newspapers of general circulation in the county. Hearing may not be held less than one month or more than 3 months from the date of the filing of the petition. It is unlawful to assume a different name except by court proceedings. A divorced woman may resume her maiden name by filing acknowledged notice (statement) with the prothonotary of the court where the divorce was entered.
Basic Form required for filing: Verified Petition; Order Directing Notice of Petition and Setting Date for Hearing; Notice of Petition; Decree Granting Name change.
STATUTE: Pa. Stat. Ann. Tit. 54,§1-6 (1964) 25,§623-4(b) (1969) (elections), 57,§156 (1964) (notary)

RHODE ISLAND: Petition to change the names of a person is filed in the Probate Court.
Basic Form required for filing: Verified Petition; Order Granting Change of Name.
STATUTE: R.I. Gen. Laws. Ann. §8-9-9 (1970) §15-7-4 (1970) (adoption), §15-7-15 (1970) (adoption)

SOUTH CAROLINA: Petition is presented to a judge of the Circuit Court of the petitioner's county of residence. No publication is required, and, in general, except for instances when the reasons for the proposed change of name are suspicious or questionable, no hearings are required as well, especially in adult petitions.
Basic Form required for filing: Verified Petition; Order Granting Change of Name.
STATUTE: S. Car. Code Ann. §48-51 to §48-55 (1962, Supp. 1971), §10-2584 (1962) (adoption), §15-1382 1962 (adoption), §20-5.2 (1962) (legitimacy)

SOUTH DAKOTA: Petition is filed in the Circuit Court of petitioner's county of residence; petitioner must be a resident of the county of filing for at least 6 months prior to the filing of the petition. Notice of hearing must be

78

published once each week for two consecutive weeks.
Basic Form required for filing: Verified Petition; Notice of Hearing; Order Granting Change of Name.
STATUTE: S.D. Compiled Laws Ann. §21-37-1 to §21-37-10 (1967, 1972 Supp.), §12-4-18 (1967) (elections)

TENNESSEE: Application is made to the appropriate Circuit, Chancery, Probate, or County Court for the county of the petitioner's residence, depending on the county of filing. A hearing date is set at which the petitioner appears. Following the hearing before the hearing officer, who may be a judge or a court clerk or master of court, the order authorizing the change will be signed.
Basic Form required for filing: Verified Petition; Order Granting Change of Name.
STATUTE: Tenn. Code Ann. §23-801 to §23.805 (1955, 1972 Supp.), §36-304 (1955) (legitimacy), §36-105 (1972 Supp.) (adoption)

TEXAS: For an adult petition, the application is filed in the District Court of the petitioner's county of residence, and in the Family Court if it's for a minor's application. No publication or hearing is usually required, and the judge will generally sign the order approving the name change if he or she is satisfied that it is "for the interest or benefit of the applicant to so change his name".
Basic Form required for filing: Verified Petition; Order Granting Change of Name.
STATUTE: Tex. Rev. Civil Stat. Art. 5928-5931 (1962)

UTAH: Petition is filed in the District Court of petitioner's county of residence; petitioner must be a resident of the county of filing for at least one year prior to the filing of the petition. The court may, in its discretion, order petitioner to give notice of the hearing to designated parties.
Basic Form required for filing: Verified Petition; Notice of Hearing; Order Granting Change of Name.
STATUTE: Utah Code Ann. §42-1-1, 42-1-3 (1970), §78-30-10 (1953) (adoption)

VERMONT: A "declaration" (a statement) proclaiming change of name is signed, sealed and acknowledged before a judge of the Probate Court in the district of the petitioner's residence. A married person must have the consent of the spouse in such document, who must also sign, seal and acknowledge it. The change of name by a married man (wherein the declaration fully sets forth the names, places and dates of birth of the wife and minor children) automatically changes the names of the wife and minor children listed. Minor's petition is signed by the adult parent or guardian acting for him, but if the minor is over 14 years of age, he must himself give his consent (in writing) to the petition. Notice of filing of petition is published in appropriate newspaper for three successive weeks.
Basic Form required for filing: Verified Declaration (Sworn

Statement); Notice of Filing Petition; Order Granting Change of Name.
STATUTE: Vt. Stat. Ann. Tit. 15, §811-816 (1958, Supp. 1972), tit. 15, §431 (1958) (adoption)

VIRGINIA: Application is filed in the Circuit Court of the county or city in which the petitioner resides. A minor's application is made on his behalf by the parent, guardian or next friend; if one of the parents is living but does not join in or consent to the petition, he (or she) should be served with notice of the application, and should he object to the change, a hearing is held by the court before a final determination is made on the granting of the change. The Court will authorize the change, unless it considers that the change is sought "for a fraudulent purpose or would otherwise infringe upon the rights of other, or, in (the) case of a minor, that the change of name is not in the best interest of the minor."
Basic Form required for filing: Verified Petition; Order Granting Change of Name.
STATUTE: Code of Va. Art. 20, #8.01-217, #24.1-51 (1972 Supp.) (elections)

WASHINGTON: Petition is filed in the Superior Court of the petitioner's county of residence; adult petitioner may request the change of name of his child or ward. No publication or the giving of public notice is required to be made. Petitioner appears in person before the judge to file the petition, and the petition may be signed the same time and place authorizing the change.
Basic Form required for filing: Verified Petition; Order Granting Change of Name.
STATUTE: Wash. Rev. Code Ann. §4.24.130 (1962), §29.10.050 (1965) (elections)

WEST VIRGINIA: Petition is filed in the Circuit Court of petitioner's county of residence, or any other court of record thereof having jurisdiction for such county. Petitioner must be a bona fide resident of the county of filing for at least one year prior to the filing of the petition. <u>Before</u> filing the petition, the petitioner must first have a notice of the **proposed** petition published giving the time and place that the application will be made; such publication is to be made in a "Class 1 legal advertisement" in a newspaper published in the county of filing of the petition. Any person having objections to the proposed change of name may appear at the time and place named in the notice, and shall be heard in opposition to such change. Following the publication and the hearing (if any was had), the court may order the change of name applied for, providing it finds that no injury will be done to any person by the change, that proper and reasonable cause exists for making the change, and that the change is not desired for any "fraudulent or evil intent" by the petitioner.
Basic Form required for filing: Verified Petition; Notice of filing Petition; Order Granting Change of Name.
STATUTE: W. Vir. Code Ann. §48-5-1 to §48-5-6 (1966, 1972

Supp.), §48-4-1 (1972 Supp.) (adoption)

WISCONSIN: Petitioner is filed in the Circuit Court of the petitioner's county of residence. For minors under 14 years of age, the petition is made on their behalf by the parents or guardian. Following the filing of the petition, the judge will sign an order authorizing the giving of a notice of the petition and of the hearing thereof, by publication. The said notice is then published in a county newspaper for 3 successive weeks prior to the hearing date. Following the hearing, the judge signs the order authorizing the name change. Changing of name is restricted in respect to petitioners practicing a profession under a license (except for public school teachers) unless a hearing establishes that no detriment will result in such a change. Copy of name change order is filed (by the clerk of court) with the registrar of deeds and with the registrar of vital statistics, if petitioner was born in the state; and the birth and marriage records, if petitioner was born and married in Wisconsin, shall also be corrected by the state registrar to show the new name.
Basic Form required for filing: Verified Petition; Notice of Hearing; Order for Hearing; Order Granting Change of Name.
STATUTE: Wis. Stat. Ann. Sec. 786.36-786.37 §48.91(Supp. 1972) (adoption).

WYOMING: Petition is filed in the District Court of the petitioner's county of residence; petitioner must be a resident of the county for at least 2 years prior to the filing of the petition. Public notice of the making of the petition is to be given in the same manner as service by publication on non-residents is done in civil actions.
Basic Form required for filing: Verified Petition; Notice of Filing Petition; Order Granting Change of Name.
STATUTE: Wyom Stat. Ann. §1-739 to §1-742 (1959)

APPENDIX C
HOW TO GET BIRTH AND
DEATH RECORDS

A common (though by no means universal) requirement made of persons who file name change applications, is to demand of them that they submit their birth (or death) certificate - a "certified" or an original copy thereof, among other documentation s.

An official certificate of birth should be on file in the locality where the event occurred. The Federal Government does not maintain files. These records are filed permanently either in a State vital statistics office or in a city, county, or other local office. To obtain a certified copy of your birth certificate, write or go to the vital statistics office of the State you were born.

To ensure that you receive an accurate record of your birth certificate, please follow the steps outlined below:

- Write to the appropriate office to have your request filled. (See sample letter on p.85)
- For all certificates, send a money order or certified check because the office cannot refund cash lost in transit. All fees are subject to change.
- Type or print all names and addresses in the letter.
- Give the following information.
    1. Full name of person whose record is being requested.
    2. Sex and race.
    3. Parents' name, including maiden name of mother.
    4. Month, day, and year of birth.
    5. Place of birth (city or town, county, and State; and name of hospital, if any.)
    6. Purpose for which copy is needed.
    7. Relationship to person whose record is being requested.

Addresses To Apply To In Each Of The States

Place of Event	Address
ALABAMA Birth or Death	Bureau of Vital Statistics State Department of Public Health Montgomery, AL 36130
ALASKA Birth or Death	Department of Health and Social Services Bureau of Vital Statistics Pouch H-02G Juneau, AK 99811
AMERICAN SAMOA Birth or Death	Registrar of Vital Statistics Vital Statistics Section Government of American Samoa Pago Pago, AS 96799
ARIZONA Birth or Death	Vital Records Section Arizona Department of Health Services P.O. Box 3887 Phoenix, AZ 85030
ARKANSAS Birth or Death	Division of Vital Records Arkansas Department of Health 4815 West Markham Street Little Rock, AR 72201
CALIFORNIA Birth or Death	Vital Statistics Branch Department of Health Services 410 N Street Sacramento, CA 95814
CANAL ZONE Birth or Death	Panama Canal Commission Vital Statistics Clerk APO Miami 34011
COLORADO Birth or Death	Vital Records Section Colorado Department of Health 4210 East 11th Avenue Denver, CO 80220
CONNECTICUT Birth or Death	Department of Health Services Vital Records Section Division of Health Statistics 79 Elm Street Hartford, CT 06115
DELAWARE Birth or Death	Bureau of Vital Statistics Division of Public Health Department of Health and Social Services State Health Building Dover, DE 19901

Place of Event	Address
DISTRICT OF COLUMBIA Birth or Death	Vital Records Branch 615 Pennsylvania Avenue Washington, D.C. 20004
FLORIDA Birth or Death	Department of Health and Rehabilitative Services Office of Vital Statistics P.O. Box 210 Jacksonville, FL 32231
GEORGIA Birth or Death	Georgia Department of Human Resources Vital Records Unit Room 217-H 47 Trinity Avenue, SW Atlanta, GA 30334
GUAM Birth or Death	Office of Vital Statistics Department of Public Health and Social Services Government of Guam P.O. Box 2816 Agana, GU, M.I. 96910
HAWAII Birth or Death	Research and Statistics Office State Department of Health P.O. Box 3378 Honolulu, HI 96801
IDAHO Birth or Death	Bureau of Vital Statistics, Standards, and Local Health Services State Department of Health and Welfare Statehouse Boise, ID 83720
ILLINOIS Birth or Death	Office of Vital Records State Department of Public Health 535 West Jefferson Street Springfield, IL 62761
INDIANA Birth or Death	Division of Vital Records State Board of Health 1330 West Michigan Street P.O. Box 1964 Indianapolis, IN 46206
IOWA Birth or Death	Iowa State Department of Health Vital Records Section Lucas State Office Building Des Moines. IA 50319

Place of Event	Address	Place of Event	Address
KANSAS Birth or Death	Bureau of Registration and Health Statistics Kansas State Department of. Health and Environment 6700 South Topeka Avenue Topeka, KS 66620	**MISSOURI** Birth or Death	Division of Health Bureau of Vital Records State Department of Health and Welfare Jefferson City, MO 65101
KENTUCKY Birth or Death	Office of Vital Statistics Department for Human Resources 275 East Main Street Frankfort, KY 40621	**MONTANA** Birth or Death	Bureau of Records and Statistics State Department of Health and Environmental Sciences Helena, MT 59601
LOUISIANA Birth or Death	Division of Vital Records Office of Health Services and Environmental Quality P.O. Box 60630 New Orleans, LA 70160	**NEBRASKA** Birth or Death	Bureau of Vital Statistics State Department of Health 301 Centennial Mall South P.O. Box 95007 Lincoln, NE 68509
MAINE Birth or Death	Office of Vital Records Human Services Building Station II State House Augusta, ME 04333	**NEVADA** Birth or Death	Division of Health-Vital Statistics Capitol Complex Carson City, NV 89710
MARYLAND Birth or Death	Division of Vital Records State Department of Health and Mental Hygiene State Office Building P.O. Box 13146 201 West Preston Street Baltimore, MD 21703	**NEW HAMPSHIRE** Birth or Death	Bureau of Vital Records Health and Welfare Building Hazen Drive Concord, NH 03301
MASSACHUSETTS Birth or Death	Registry of Vital Records and Statistics 150 Tremont Street Room B-3 Boston, MA 02111	**NEW JERSEY** Birth or Death	State Department of Health Bureau of Vital Statistics CN 360 Trenton, NJ 08625 Archives and History Bureau State Library Division State Department of Education Trenton, NJ 08625
MICHIGAN Birth or Death	Office of Vital and Health Statistics Michigan Department of Public Health 3500 North Logan Street Lansing, MI 48914	**NEW MEXICO** Birth or Death	Vital Statistics Bureau New Mexico Health Services Division P.O. Box 968 Santa Fe, NM 87503
		NEW YORK Birth or Death	Bureau of Vital Records State Department of Health Empire State Plaza Tower Building Albany, NY 12237
MINNESOTA Birth or Death	Minnesota Department of Health Section of Vital Statistics 717 Delaware Street SE Minneapolis, MN 55440	**NEW YORK CITY** Birth or Death	Bureau of Vital Records Department of Health of New York City 125 Worth Street New York, NY 10013
MISSISSIPPI Birth or Death	Vital Records State Board of Health P.O. Box 1700 Jackson, MS 39205	**NORTH CAROLINA** Birth or Death	Department of Human Resources Division of Health Services Vital Records Branch P.O. Box 2091 Raleigh, NC 27602

Place of Event	Address
NORTH DAKOTA Birth or Death	Division of Vital Records State Department of Health Office of Statistical Services Bismarck, ND 58505
OHIO Birth or Death	Division of Vital Statistics Ohio Department of Health G-20 Ohio Departments Bldg. 65 South Front Street Columbus, OH 43215
OKLAHOMA Birth or Death	Vital Records Section State Department of Health Northeast 10th Street & Stonewall P.O. Box 53551 Oklahoma City, OK 73152
OREGON Birth or Death	Oregon State Health Division Vital Statistics Section P.O. Box 116 Portland, OR 97207
PENNSYLVANIA Birth or Death	Division of Vital Records Pennsylvania Department of Health P.O. Box 1528 New Castle, PA 16103
PUERTO RICO Birth or Death	Division of Demographic Registry and Vital Statistics Department of Health San Juan, PR 00908
RHODE ISLAND Birth or Death	Division of Vital Statistics State Department of Health Room 101, Cannon Building 75 Davis Street Providence, RI 02908
SOUTH CAROLINA Birth or Death	Office of Vital Records and Public Health Statistics S.C. Department of Health and Environmental Control 2600 Bull Street Columbia, SC 29201
SOUTH DAKOTA Birth or Death	State Department of Health Health Statistics Program Joe Foss Office Building Pierre, SD 57501
TENNESSEE Birth or Death	Division of Vital Records State Department of Public Health Cordell Hull Building Nashville, TN 37219
TEXAS Birth or Death	Bureau of Vital Statistics Texas Department of Health 1100 West 49th Street Austin, TX 78756

Place of Event	Address
TRUST TERRITORY OF THE PACIFIC ISLANDS Birth or Death	Director of Medical Services Department of Medical Services Saipan, Mariana Islands 96950
UTAH Birth or Death	Bureau of Health Statistics Utah Department of Health 150 West North Temple P.O. Box 2500 Salt Lake City, UT 84110
VERMONT Birth or Death	Vermont Department of Health Vital Records Section Box 70 115 Colchester Avenue Burlington, VT 05401
VIRGINIA Birth or Death	Division of Vital Records and Health Statistics State Department of Health James Madison Building P.O. Box 1000 Richmond, VA 23208
VIRGIN ISLANDS (U.S.) Birth or Death St. Croix	Registrar of Vital Statistics Charles Harwood Memorial Hospital St. Croix, VI 00820
St. Thomas and St. John	Registrar of Vital Statistics Charlotte Amalie St. Thomas, VI 00802
WASHINGTON Birth or Death	Vital Records P.O. Box 9709, LB11 Olympia, WA 98504
WEST VIRGINIA Birth or Death	Division of Vital Statistics State Department of Health State Office Building No. 3 Charleston, WV 25305
WISCONSIN Birth or Death	Bureau of Health Statistics Wisconsin Division of Health P.O. Box 309 Madison, WI 53701
WYOMING Birth or Death	Vital Records Services Division of Health and Medical Services Hathaway Building Cheyenne, WY 82002

LETTER TO OBTAIN BIRTH / DEATH CERTIFICATE (A SAMPLE)

My Name: _____
My Address: _____
Date: _____ 19 ____

(Name & address from Appendix C)
TO: _____
      _____

To the Director for Records:

I am writing to request a birth certificate for one whose name at birth is _____
_____, bearing the birth certificate No. _____. The said child (or party) was
born on or about the _____ day of the month of _____ 19, _____, and the following are the
relevant particulars:

His (her) father's name: _____
His (her) mother's name: _____
City/County & State of birth: _____
Hospital where born: _____
Other available data of relevance: _____

I am in need of a certified copy of the birth certificate for the following reasons or purposes:
(specify the reasons)

Enclosed, please find a check (money order) in the amount of $_____ to cover the charge for
this service. Should there be any additional costs or information required, please contact me.

Sincerely yours,

_____
(My signature)

My Name (printed) _____

APPENDIX **D**

SAMPLES OF SOME MISCELLANEOUS OTHER
FORMS OF DIFFERENT STATES USABLE IN NAME CHANGES

The following additional forms listed below, are reproduced in this chapter as representative illustrative samples of name change forms. Many of them are national forms, usable for general filings, in just about every state, while others are state-specific — representing the special version of the forms applicable to particular states.

NOTE: For complete list of <u>all</u> forms employed in this manual, see Appendix A.

(ORDER TO SHOW CAUSE—CALIFORNIA VERSION)

The _____ Court of the State/ City of
_____, in and for the County of
_____, State of _____

Index No. _____

Re: Matter of the Application of (*(present name to be changed)* To Change His/Her Name to: *(proposed name, in full)*)

ORDER TO SHOW CAUSE WHY PETITION SHOULD NOT BE GRANTED

On the reading and filing of the verified petition of [*the petitioner's name, in full*], petitioner, praying for an order to change the name of [*full present name to be changed*] to [*proposed name, in full*], and good cause appearing for same,

IT IS HEREBY ORDERED, that:

1. All persons who may be affected or prejudiced by the change of name, or may otherwise be interested in the said matter, appear before this court at the following date, time and address: [*enter the court's address, date and time set for hearing*], to show cause, if any, why the petition should not be granted; and

2. A copy of this Order-to-Show-Cause [and of the verified petition]*be published in the following newspaper (leave blank for clerk to fill in)   [or, be served by certified mail to the following persons (*leave blank for clk. to fill in*)], a newspaper of general circulation published in the county of _____, state of _____, for [*specify the number of times, as required by your local rules*] successive weeks from the date of such publication to the date set above for the hearing.

Date:_____   Signed:_____
                                                    Judge of the court

---

* Requiring that the petition, itself, be published is not common, and is generally required in only a tiny handful of jurisdictions. Strike this out and do not include, if not necessary.

(NOTICE—NATIONAL VERSION)

IN THE _____ COURT OF THE STATE OF _____ -
IN AND FOR THE COUNTY OF _____,
Holding at this address:_____

Re: Matter of the Application of:
_____, for him/her,
    (Petitioner)
or a Minor, ___(His/Her present name, in full)_____,
To assume the Name:
___(the proposed name in full)_____

Index
Docket No._____

NOTICE OF PETITION / HEARING

TO: _(Name & address of the party being notified)_
_____

    You are hereby notified that:

    An application (petition) was filed (will be filed) in the above designated court by the undersigned person on the _____ day of _____ 19 _____, praying for an Order/Judgement of the Court authorizing petitioner, or a minor child named, __(present name of child, in full)__ to assume another name as: __(proposed name, in full)_____ .

    The said petition (application) will come before the said court for hearing at the courthouse thereof on the _____ day of _____ 19 _____, at 9:30 A.M. of the said date in Room _____ thereof, or as soon thereafter as the parties can be heard.

    Any person desiring to object to the granting of the petition may do so by filing an objection in writing with the clerk of the above entitled court no later than this date: _____, and by thereafter appearing at the said hearing at the appointed time and place.

Today's Date:_____

My Present Name: _(Petitioner's present name, in full)_
My Address: _____
_____

ORDER GRANTING CHANGE OF FAMILY NAME
(NATIONAL VERSION)

The _____ Court of the State/City of _____
In and for the county of _____, State of _____

Index No._____

Re: Matter of the Application of: _____
_____, To
Change the Name Of _____
to the Name _____

ORDER GRANTING CHANGE OF FAMILY NAME
(short form)

On reading and filing the verified petition of _____, requesting that his surname, the surname of the wife **[her full name],** and the surname of the minor child, named and aged as follows: _____ be changed by order of this court from _____ to _____; and,

it appearing to the satisfaction of this court that notice of the petition was duly published, (and/or, duly served upon all parties required), that the reasons for such proposed change of name are good and sufficient and are not for fraudulent or wrongful purposes, and that others will not be prejudiced or harmed by it,

IT IS ORDERED that the surname of petitioner, _____, and his wife, _____ [her full *name*], and the minor children [their full names], be changed from _____[the present surname] to _____, and that subsequently they shall bear and be known by the surname of __**[proposed name]**

Date: _____ 19 _____

Signed: _____
(Judge)

(PETITION TO PREVENT - NATIONAL VERSION)

THE _____ COURT OF THE CITY/STATE OF _____

COUNTY OF _____
STATE OF _____

[Name of the petitioning party]
Plaintiff / Petitioner -against -
[Name of the party being sued]
Defendant / Respondent

VERIFIED PETITION TO PREVENT MINOR'S MOTHER FROM ALLOWING CHILD TO USE ANOTHER'S SURNAME

INDEX NO. _____

1.   I, the undersigned petitioner, am the father of *[the full present name of the minor child]*, a minor child who is _____ years of age, and I make this petition for an injunction by the court to bar the said child's mother, namely, *[enter name of the minor's mother]*, from allowing the child to use the stepfather's surname.

2.   I currently reside at this address *[enter same, including the city, county and state]*; petitioner and the child's mother, the respondent herein, were divorced on or about this date:_____ 19 _____, and our said child has been in the care and custody of the respondent since the said divorce pursuant to the terms of the divorce decree.

3.   Respondent has since remarried to a man believed to be named *[enter name of the minor's stepfather]*.

4.   Upon information and belief, the respondent has asked the *child's [enter details, as applicable, e.g. "school teachers"]* and other members of the community to call the minor child by a different surname, namely *[enter stepfather's surname]*, believed to be the name of the minor's stepfather, the present husband of the respondent herein.

5.   The minor's name was never legally changed by a court order, nor has the stepfather adopted him/her.

6.   I have been very close to my son (daughter) since his birth, and the love and affection and fondness we share for each other has been demonstrably mutual between my son and I to this day.

7.   Since the said divorce between my son's (daughter's) mother and I, I have consistently paid her the sum of $_____ every week/month for the support and maintenance of the child, the amount stipulated by the divorce judgment; furthermore, I have equally exercised the rights of visitation with my son and visited him regularly. At all times, and in varying ways, I have always had genuine parental love for and interest in the child.

8.   Based upon information and belief, the plan to change my son's name so that he may answer a different name from mine is really a vindictive design on the part of his mother to drive a wedge of division between my son and I and thereby thwart the healthy family relationship existing between a father and son.

WHEREFORE, petitioner requests an order of this court enjoining the respondent from allowing or encouraging the said minor child to be known by any other surname except his birth surname, namely, **[the child's original name]**, and for such further relief as the court may deem just and equitable.

State of _____,
County of _____, ss.:

Signed: **[objecting father's name]**
Same Name (printed) X_____

Before me, a duly qualified Notary Public of the State of _____, appeared Mr./Mrs. _____, to me known, and known to me to be the individual described in the within instrument, and who signed, acknowledged and swore to the said instrument as true, on this _____ day of _____ 19 _____

_____
(Notary Public's seal)

(PETITION OF OBJECTION - NATIONAL VERSION)

The _____ Court of the State/City of _____
In and for the County   of _____ State of _____

Index No._____

Re: Matter of the Application of *[adult petitioner's name]* for Leave of Court to Change the Name of *[Minor's full present Name]* to the Name *[minor's proposed name]*

Petition of Objecting Father in Opposition to Minor's Change of Name

1.   I, the undersigned intervenor, am the father of *[full, present name of the minor child]*, the minor child whose name is sought to be changed herein by a certain petition filed with and now pending in this court, and I reside at this address: _____, in the city of _____, county of _____, state of _____.

2.   I hereby assert my vigorous opposition to the proposed change of name for my son (daughter); such a change will be detrimental to the best interests of the child, the reasons for this being as follows: *[Set forth the basis of your opposition, the likely effect of such change on your relationship with the child, and the like. Could read something like paragraphs 3 and 4 below, for example, if applicable. See, also, p.8-12 for more pointers.]*

3.   I have been very close to my son (daughter) since he was born, and the love and affection and fondness we share for each other has been demonstrably mutual between my son and I to this day, and the plan to change my son's name so that he may answer a different name from mine is really a vindictive design on the part of his mother to drive a wedge of division between my son and I and thereby thwart the healthy family relationship existing between a father and son.

4.   Since my divorce (or separation) from my son's mother on or about the month of _____ 19 _____, following which she gained the physical custody of my son, I have consistently paid her the sum of $_____ every week/month for the support and maintenance of the child, as required by the divorce judgement; furthermore, I have equally exercised the rights of visitation with my son and visited with him regularly. At all times, and in varying ways, I have always had genuine parental love for and interest in the child, and at no time have I ever shown or even hinted at a desire to abandon the child.

5.   WHEREFORE, I respectfully request that the application to change the name of my son (daughter) from his present birth name, which is, _____, to the said proposed new name, be denied in its entirety.

Signed: *[objecting party's name]*
Same Name in Full (printed):_____

State of _____, ss:
County of _____,

Before me, a duly qualified Notary Public of the State of _____, appeared Mr./Mrs. _____, to me known, or made known to me to be the individual described in the within instrument, and who signed, acknowledged and swore to the said instrument as true, on this _____ day of _____19 _____

_____
(Notary Public's seal)

(PETITION - FLORIDA VERSION)

IN THE CIRCUIT/CHANCERY COURT FOR
_____ **COUNTY, FLORIDA**

File No. _____

IN RE: THE PETITION OF:

_____ ,

To Change Said Name to:

_____ ,

PETITION FOR CHANGE OF NAME

The Petition of _____ and _____ , shows:

1. This is a petition for a change of name of Petitioner(s) and (None) _____ .

2. Petitioner(s) is/are bona fide resident(s) of the County of _____ , in Florida, at this address: _____ .

3. Petitioner(s) was/were born on the _____ day of _____ 19 _____ , in the city and state of _____ , and has/have resided since birth at these cities and states: _____ . Petitioner's father's name is _____ ; Petitioner's mother's maiden name is _____ .

4. The marital status of petitioner is: single/married to _____ ; Petitioner has the following children named, aged, and resident as follows: _____ _____ .

5. Petitioner's name has previously been changed by court order in this Court and date: (None) _____ .

6. Petitioner is presently employed as _____ , with the following employer _____ , and for the past five years he/she has been employed as follows: _____ .

7. Petitioner has been known by no other name other than as shown in paragraph 4 above, except: None.

8. Petitioner has not been adjudicated a bankrupt or convicted of a felony, except _____ _____ ; no money judgment has ever been entered against petitioner, and he/she has no criminal record, except _____ .

9. This petition is not filed for an ulterior or illegal purpose and the granting of the petition will not in any manner invade the property rights of others, whether partnership, patent, good will, privacy, trademark or otherwise.

WHEREFORE, petitioner(s) demand that their present name, as aforementioned, be changed to:

_____

Upon penalties of perjury, I (we) the undersigned, declare that I (we) have read the foregoing, and that the facts alleged therein are true.

SWORN TO BEFORE ME,
on this _____ day of
_____ 19 _____ .

SIGNED: _____ (His/Her present name, in full)
                                                                                    Petitioner

_____
(Notary Public)

_____ (Present name, in full)
                                                                                    Petitioner

My Commission Expires:

(FINAL JUDGMENT - FLORIDA VERSION)

IN THE CIRCUIT/CHANCERY COURT FOR
_____COUNTY, FLORIDA

File No. _____

In Re: THE PETITION OF:

_____,

To Change Said Name to:

_____,

FINAL JUDGMENT OF NAME CHANGE

THIS ACTION was heard before the Court on the sworn Petition of the above-named petitioner(s) for a change of name.

Upon the evidence submitted and/or presented, it is ADJUDGED that the name(s) of the within petitioner (s) _____, is/are herewith changed to _____.

ORDERED at _____, Florida, on this date _____.

_____
Circuit Judge

Copies furnished to: _____

(PETITION - LOUISIANA VERSION)

_____

_____, Petitioner,

-versus-

_____ District
Attorney

DISTRICT COURT,
_____**JUDICIAL DISTRICT,**
PARISH OF _____
STATE OF LOUISIANA

Case No. _____

PETITION FOR CHANGE OF NAME_ (Adult/Minor)

The Petition of the above-named petitioner whose present full name(s) is, _____
_____, and who is domiciled in the Parish of _____, Louisiana, respectfully
shows the Honorable Court that:

1. Petitioner wishes to change his/her name (or the minor child's name)*, from _____
_____, to another name, namely, _____ , pursuant to the
provisions of LSA R.S. 13:4751.

2. Petitioner wishes to change his/her name (or the minor child's name)* for the following reasons:
_____ he/she* prefers the proposed name(s), to the present name(s)_____.

3. The following are personal information pertaining to the said petitioner (minor child)* herein:

My (the Minor's)* Date of Birth:_____
My (the Minor's)* Sex:_____
My (the Minor's)* Address:_____
My (the Minor's)* Place of Birth is: City _____ State _____
My (the Minor's)* Father's Name is: _____
My (the Minor's)* Mother's Maiden Name is: _____
My (the Minor's)* Social Security Number is: _____ - _____ - _____

WHEREFORE, petitioner prays that the district attorney for this Parish be cited and commanded to appear
and answer this petition and, after all due proceedings, that there be judgment changing petitioner's/minor's*
name from the present name, as set forth above, to the above proposed new name.

SIGNED:_____
Petitioner's Present Names, in Full

Address:_____

* Neatly cross out one or the other inapplicable term or word, and cross out the terms contained within the
brackets, if petition is not for change of a minor's name.

(ANSWER TO PETITION - LOUISIANA VERSION)

```
_____

_____, Petitioner,

           -versus-

_____ District
                         Attorney
```

DISTRICT COURT,
_____ JUDICIAL DISTRICT
PARISH OF _____
STATE OF LOUISIANA

Case No. _____

ANSWER TO PETITION FOR NAME CHANGE

NOW INTO COURT COMES Mr./Mrs./Ms. _____, the District Attorney of the _____ Parish of Louisiana, who, as and for the Answer to the Petition of the above-designated Petitioner, respectfully states as follows:

1. The undersigned, the District Attorney or the authorized representative herein, has no objection to urge against the change of name of the petitioner (minor chil (ren)*, from _____ to _____.

WHEREFORE, the undersigned prays that there be such judgment as the law and the evidence may warrant.

SIGNED: _____(leave blank for his/her signature)_____
                    (District Attorney)

Full Name of District Attorney:_____(leave blank)_____

Address:_____
_____Phone # (   )_____

---

*Cross out the term contained within the bracket, if petition is <u>not</u> for change of a minor's name.

(JUDGMENT (Order) - LOUISIANA VERSION)

Copyright © 1998
DO-IT-YOURSELF LEGAL PUBLISHERS
Newark, N.J.

PETITION FOR NAME CHANGE OF:

_____,Petitioner,

-versus-

_____,District
Attorney.

DISTRICT COURT,
_____**JUDICIAL DISTRICT**
PARISH OF _____
STATE OF LOUISIANA

Case No. _____

JUDGMENT FOR CHANGE OF NAME

CONSIDERING the petition and the answer filed herein on the within matter, and the law and the evidence being in favor of the petitioner;

IT IS ORDERED, ADJUDGED, AND DECREED, that the petitioner's (minor child's)* name, _____, be and hereby is changed to _____ , and that he/she henceforth be known by this name as his/her* true and lawful name.

Petitioner's (the Minor's)* Present Name is:_____

Petitioner's (the Minor's)* Date of Birth is:_____

Petitioner's (the Minor's)* Address is:_____

Petitioner's (the Minor's)* Sex is:_____

Petitioner's (the Minor's)* Place of Birth is: City _____ State _____

Petitioner's (the Minor's)* Father's Name is: _____

Petitioner's (the Minor's)* Mother's Maiden Name is: _____

Petitioner's (the Minor's)* Social Security Number is: _____ - _____ - _____

JUDGMENT READ, RENDERED AND SIGNED at _____, Louisiana, on this _____ day of _____ , 19 _____.

_____
JUDGE

*Neatly Cross out the term contained within the bracket, if petition is not for change of a minor's name.

(NOTICE - NEW JERSEY VERSION

Copyright © 1990, 1997
DO-IT-YOURSELF LEGAL PUBLISHERS
Newark, N.J.

RE: Matter of the Application of:

_____ For

Him/Her, or a Minor, _____

_____, To Assume the name:

_____

SUPERIOR COURT OF NEW JERSEY
COUNTY OF _____
LAW DIVISION - CIVIL ACTION

Docket No. _____

NOTICE OF APPLICATION FOR NAME CHANGE

TO WHOM IT MAY CONCERN:

    Take Notice that the undersigned, will apply to the Superior Court of the State of New Jersey, for the County of _____ at the County Courthouse thereof, on the _____ day of _____ 19, _____, at 9 o'clock in the afternoon of the said date, at the Court House in the City of _____, New Jersey, for a Judgment authorizing the said petitioner, or a minor, named, _____, to assume another name, namely, the name of: **(proposed name, in full)**

My Present Name: _____

Address: _____

        _____

NOTE: This Notice is specifically the version used by the State of New Jersey in its procedures. The essence (substance) of such forms is just about the same for most states.

(ORDER - NEW JERSEY VERSION)

(Adult)

PETITIONER'S NAME: _____

Address:_____

RE: Matter of the Application of:

_____ for him/

her, or a Minor, _____ ,

To Assume the name: _____

SUPERIOR COURT OF NEW JERSEY

COUNTY OF _____

LAW DIVISION - CIVIL ACTION

Docket No. _____

ORDER SETTING DATE
FOR HEARING (Name Change)

Upon the Application/Petition of Mr./Mrs./Ms. **(Petitioner's name in full)** _____

_____, the Petitioner herein appearing pro se, made to this Court for a Judgment authorizing said Petitioner, or a Minor, to Assume the name as set forth above, and for the entry of an Order Fixing a date for the hearing of such application;

it is, on this date, the _____ day of _____ 19 _____, ORDERED that the following be fixed as the time and place for the hearing of such application and any objections that may be made thereto, namely: the _____ day of _____ 19 _____, at 9 o'clock in the afternoon, or as soon thereafter as the matter can be heard, in the Courthouse in the City of _____, County of _____, State of New Jersey; and it is further

(Judge fills this in)

ORDERED, that a Notice of the said application/petition for Name Change be published in this newspaper **(court fill this in)**, _____ once, and that such publication be made at least two calendar weeks preceding the date set above for the hearing.

ENTER:_____**(Judge signs here)**_____

Judge

NOTE: This ORDER is the version used by the State of New Jersey in its procedures.

Copyright © 1990, 1997
DO-IT-YOURSELF LEGAL PUBLISHERS
Newark, N.J.

(MOTION - MARYLAND VERSION)

IN THE __Circuit__ Court of the State of __Maryland__
In and For the County of _____

RE: APPLICATION OF ____(your present name, in full)___

    TO CHANGE THE NAME OF: _____

    TO: _____(proposed name, in full)_____

Index No. _____

MOTION FOR ORDER TO POST (PUBLISH)

    The undersigned Petitioner for a Change of Name, moves the Court for an Order requiring and causing a Sheriff of the County/Parish of ____(county of filing)___ in the within state, to post a Notice of Posting of the within filed Petitioner's Petition for Name Change on the Bulletin Board of the county courthouse herein for a period of _____ days/weeks, pursuant to the rules of court for change of name.

    Petitioner's affidavit (Petition/application) in support of this motion, and a copy of the Notice of Posting are herewith annexed.

SIGNED: __(Sign here—in full—present name)__
(Petitioner)

ORDER FOR POSTING
(Change of Name)

    UPON the motion of __(your present name, in full)__, the above-named Petitioner/ Applicant, herewith annexed; it is hereby

    ORDERED that the Sheriff of the County of _____ of this State shall post in a public place, on the Bulletin Board in the County Courthouse herein, a Notion of within filed Petitioner's petition for Name Change, for the required period of time (for a period of _____ days/weeks/months.)

DATED:_____ _____(Judge sings here)_____
                                Judge

NOTE: The above two forms are the versions employed under the State of Maryland's procedures.

100
(AFFIDAVIT OF GOOD CHARACTER - NORTH CAROLINA)

Copyright © 1990, 1997
Do-IT-YOURSELF LEGAL PUBLISHERS
Newark, N.J.

RE: For, _____ (name of the petitioner) _____ .

Index No._____

AFFIDAVIT TESTIFYING TO GOOD CHARACTER

STATE OF _____
COUNTY OF _____ ss.:

    MR./MRS./MS. __**(Name of the witness, in full)**__, being duly sworn, deposes and says:

1. I am over the age of eighteen (18); I am a citizen of the United States of America, and I reside at: _____, in the county of _____, State of _____ thereof; and I am fully competent to attest to the matters herein.

2. That I make this AFFIDAVIT in behalf of Mr./Mrs./Ms. __**(petitioner's present name, in full)**__, for him/her to submit with his/her Application/Petition for a Change of his/her Name by court proceedings.

3. I have personal knowledge that the said person in behalf of whom I make this representation, currently resides in this State and in the County of _____, State of _____, and that he/she has continuously resided therein for the past _____ years/months, the reason for my said knowledge being that he/she is related to me as follows (OR, I dealt with him/her in this capacity):_____

4. That in all the time that I have known the said person, I have personal knowledge and information that he/she has been a person of good moral character; during the said time I have not received any information to the contrary which would reflect adversely upon him/her.

5. That I respectfully recommend that her Application for Name Change be duly approved by the court.

               SIGNED: X (witness signs his/her full name, in presence of Notary Public)
                      (Witness)

SWORN TO BEFORE ME,
this _____ day of _____
19 _____ .

_____
      (Notary Public)

(ORDER DIRECTING NOTICE - PENNSYLVANIA VERSION)
(Adult)

PETITIONER'S NAME: _____
Address: _____

RE: Application of:

  (Petitioner's present name, in full)

FOR: **(Minor's present name, if applicable)**, Minor,
To Assume the Name: _____

IN THE COURT OF COMMON PLEAS
OF ___ **(Enter this)** ___ COUNTY,
PENNSYLVANIA

Case No. _____ **(enter this)**

ORDER DIRECTING NOTICE OF PETITION AND SETTING DATE FOR HEARING (Name Change)

Upon the verified Petition of Mr./Mrs./Ms. **(Petitioner's present name, in full)** _____
_____, the Petitioner herein appearing pro se, made to this Court for a Decree authorizing said Petitioner (or the above named Minor)* to assume another name as set forth above, and for the entry of an Order Fixing a date for the hearing of such application;

it is ORDERED, on this the _____ day of _____ 19 _____, that the following be fixed as the time and place for the hearing of such application and any objections that may be made thereto, namely: the _____ day of _____ 19 _____, at 9:30 o'clock A.M. in the morning, or as soon thereafter as the matter can be heard, in the Courthouse thereof above stated, in the City/town of _____, County of _____, Room _____ at this address: _____
_____; and it is further

ORDERED, that a Notice of the said Application/Petition for Name Change be published in these two newspapers of general circulation: _____ (leave for the court to fill in) _____, which are published in petitioner's county of residence or a contiguous county thereto, and that such publication be made and completed prior to the date set above for the hearing.

ENTER: _____
                Judge

* Cross out one or the other, as it may apply.

(PETITION - WISCONSIN VERSION)

Copyright © 1998
DO-IT-YOURSELF LEGAL PUBLISHERS
Newark, N.J.

State of Wisconsin,_____ Circuit **Court of:** _____**County.**

In the matter of the Change of Name

Case No.........................

OF:...

TO:...

PETITION FOR CHANGE

OF NAME

TO THE CIRCUIT COURT OF_____,COUNTY:_____ ss.:

The Petition of ....(Petitioner's present name, in full)................, respectfully alleges and shows to the Court:

1. That the Petitioner resides at: _____, County of _____, and is presently ....years of age, born in the city of _____, State of_____ on: _____,and is by present occupation a: _____ Social Security No. _____.

2. That the Petitioner desires a change of name

From:...; To:...

for the following reasons:...

3. That the Petitioner is not engaged in any profession for which a license has been issued by the State of Wisconsin.

4. That the Petitioner believes that the said change of name and designation will, under the circumstances, be an advantage and convenience in the Petitioner's business and his/her day-to-day activities, and further be in the Petitioner's best interest.

WHEREFORE, The Petitioner prays the Court to enter an ORDER changing the said name

of:...;

To:...

Dated at.............., Wisconsin, this .... Day of .... 19 ....

STATE OF WISCONSIN

X...
Petitioner (sign)

.... County, ss.

I, ..., being first duly sworn on oath, state that I have read the above and foregoing Petition, and know the contents thereof, and that the same is true to my own knowledge.

Subscribed and sworn to before me this
...................day of........19........

X...
Petitioner (sign)

Notary public, State of Wisconsin
My commission............................

Copyright © 1998
DO-IT-YOURSELF LEGAL PUBLISHERS
Newark, N.J.

State of Wisconsin,_____ Circuit Court of: _____County.

In the matter of the Change of Name

Case No........................

OF:...

NOTICE OF HEARING

TO:...

NOTICE IS HEREWITH GIVEN, that at a regular term of the Circuit Court of...........................
County, State of Wisconsin, on the ....day of.......................,19......, at ....o'clock.........M.,
or as soon thereafter as can be heard, there will be heard and considered the application of......................
(Petitioner's present
Name, in full)
...................., for permission to change his/her legal name and designation to:.....................................,
(Proposed name, in full)
and for consideration of any and all further matters pertaining thereto.

Dated at ...., Wisconsin, this .... Day of .... 19 ....

BY THE COURT:

(Leave blank for Judge's signature)
....
Circuit Judge

Petitioner's Name ...(Enter these information)...........

Address ....

Telephone ....

104

ORDER FOR HEARING—WISCONSIN VERSION

State of Wisconsin,_____ **Circuit Court of:** _____ **County**

In the matter of the Change of Name

Case No.........................

OF:..

TO:..

ORDER FOR HEARING

It appearing from the Petition of Mr./Mrs./Ms. ....(Petitioner's present name, in full)......., that the Petitioner
desires a change of legal name and designation to:.........(Proposed name, in full).................................

NOW, THEREFORE, on motion of said Petitioner;

IT IS ORDERED, that said Petition be heard before Branch...................... ,of the Circuit Court on

the .... Day of .... 19 ......, at ....o'clock ....M., or as soon thereafter as can be heard.

IT IS FURTHER ORDERED, that notice thereof be given by publication as a Class 3 notice for three
(3) successive weeks prior to the date of said hearing in this newspaper, named......................................,
published in .... County, Wisconsin.

Dated at ...., Wisconsin this .... Day of ....19 ......

BY THE COURT:

(Leave blank for Judge's *signature*)
....
Circuit Judge

105

Copyright © 1998
DO-IT-YOURSELF LEGAL PUBLISHERS
Newark, N.J.

State of Wisconsin,_____ **Circuit Court of:** _____ **County.**

In the matter of the Change of Name

Case No......(Enter This)...

OF:......(Petitioner's Present Name, in full)....

ORDER FOR CHANGE OF NAME

TO:......(Petitioner's Proposed Name, in full)..

The above entitled matter for a change of name was heard before the Hon. ....(clerk enters name of Judge)........, a Circuit Judge of ....County, Wisconsin, on the ....day of ....19......; and upon the Petition of ....for a change of name to: ...., and the Court having found that a notice of the time and place of the hearing on the said Petition was duly published pursuant to the Affidavit of Publication on file herein, and that the petitioner is presently ....years of age, born....................in the State of......................., and is by occupation a ....;

And the Court having further found, that the said petitioner is not engaged in any profession for which a license has been issued by the State of Wisconsin, and that the said change of name will be an advantage and convenience for the petitioner's business and his/her day-to-day activities, and will further be in the petitioner's best interests;

NOW, THEREFORE, on the motion of said Petitioner;

IT IS ORDERED, that the name of:.............(Present name of party, in full).., be changed to:.......(Proposed name, in full)...;

that this Order be entered at length upon the records of this Court and that a certified copy of said Order be filed in the offices of the Register of Deeds,.............................County, Wisconsin, and the Registrar of Vital Statistics, State of Wisconsin.

Dated at ...., Wisconsin, this .... Day of .... 19 ....

BY THE COURT:

....
Circuit Judge

Petitioner's Name ......(Present name)....................

Address ....

Telephone ....

Social Security No....................................

(ORDER /DECREE —NATIONAL VERSION)

PRESENT:

Hon. _____

Judge/ Justice

RE: Application of:

_____(adult Petitioner's name, in full)_____
FOR Leave of court to Change His/Her
Name to ___(the proposed name, in full)____ .

At a Special Term Part _____ of the _____
Court of the City/State of _____, held
in and for the County of _____, at
the county's courthouse thereof, on the _____ day of
_____ 19 _____ .

Index No. _____

ORDER/ DECREE GRANTING CHANGE OF NAME (Adult's)

The above-entitled matter came on for hearing/consideration before the undersigned Judge on the above-entered date, upon the petitioner's Application for a Change of Name which petition was dated (or sworn to) on _____ 19_____ . Upon the within annexed verified Petition, and the supporting affidavits, birth certificates, and the testimony and files and other evidence presented herewith in support of the Petitioners' application thereof, **THE COURT FINDS AS FOLLOWS:**

1. That the applicant, the subject of this petition, was born under the birth name, __(present name, in full)__ , on the _____day of_____ 19_____ , in the city of_____,County of_____, State of_____, bearing the birth Certificate No._____ .

2. That the applicant(s) has/have resided in this State and County for at least_____years_____months immediately preceding the filing of the within application, and currently resides in the County of _____, at _____-.

3. That the applicant does NOT* include any spouse or child (ren) of petitioner.

4. That the Applicant(s) desires to have his/her name changed from __(the present name, in full)__to (proposed name, in full)_____ .

5. That it appears that the application is made in good faith without intent to defraud or mislead; that the proposed change of name is not for a wrongful or evil purpose, and that no person will be injured or adversely affected or the legitimate rights thereof prejudiced or infringed upon by the proposed change of name, and that there is no reasonable objection to the proposed change of name herein.

6. That all proper statutory requirements in respect to changing of name in this state have been met, or are impracticable or are herewith dispensed with by this court.

NOW WHEREFORE, after due deliberations, it is **ORDERED**, that:

a) The petitioner, namely, __(your present name, in full)__ , is herewith authorized to assume the proposed name, __(the proposed name, in full)__ , as his/her legal name in place and in stead of the present name, effective from this date: the _____day of _____ 19_____ .

b) Petitioner shall cause this order and the petition, and all supporting papers upon which this order is granted, to be entered and/or recorded upon the records of this court promptly hereinafter.**

Dated:_____

ENTER:_____
JUDGE

---

* If, however, your spouse (and/or children) are intended to be included in the name change, then simply cross out the word "NOT" in paragraph 3, and give the original (full) names of the persons intended, and the new names to which each is to be changed.
** If the names of <u>other</u> <u>persons</u>, beside you, are also to be changed, then add additional paragraphs numbered c), d), etc to provide for the change for <u>each</u>.

APPENDIX E

SOME RELEVANT BIBLIOGRAPHY

57 <u>American</u> <u>Jurisprudence</u> 2d. Name, Sec. 10-16. A legal encyclopedia that covers all aspects of change of name law.

59 <u>American</u> <u>Jurisprudence</u> 2d, parent and child, Sec. 13

67 <u>American</u> <u>Law</u> <u>Reports</u> 3d 1266. Right of married woman to use maiden surname.

79 <u>American</u> <u>Law</u> <u>Reports</u>, 3d 562. Circumstances justifying grant or denial of petition to change adult's name.

92 <u>American</u> <u>Law</u> <u>Reports</u>, 3d 1091. Right and remedies of parents inter se with respect to the names of their children.

110 <u>American</u> <u>Law</u> <u>Reports</u>, 583. Duty and discretion of court in passing upon petition to change name of individuals.

Bander, Edward J., change of Name and Law of Names (Oceana Publications, Dobbs Ferry N.Y.:1973)

Brown, David. "Name Changes: A Rare Situation Where the Law is Easier Than You Might Think," <u>The</u> <u>People's</u> <u>Law</u> <u>Review</u>, Nolo Press (1980) pp. 69-75

Carlsson, "Surnames of Married Women and Legitimate Children," 17 <u>New</u> <u>York</u> <u>Law</u> <u>Forum</u> 552 (1971).

Change of Name in Naturalization Proceedings, 8 US Code Ann. Sec. 1447, 1454

Comments, Equal Protection of the Sexes in Kentucky: The Effect of the Hummelforf Decision in a Woman's Right to Choose Her Surname, 9 <u>Northern</u> <u>Kentucky</u> <u>Law</u> <u>Review</u>, 475 (1982)

65 <u>Corpus</u> <u>Juris</u> <u>Secundum</u>, Names. An encyclopedia (by West Publishing Company) that covers all aspects of change of name law.

Domestic relations: change of minor's surname: parental rights in minor's surname (Sobel v. Sobel—N.J.) (Marshall v. Marshall—Miss.), 44 <u>Cornell</u> <u>Law</u> <u>Quarterly</u> (1958)

Eder, Right to Choose a Name, 8 <u>Amer.</u> <u>Journal</u> <u>of</u> <u>Comparative</u> <u>Law</u> 502 (1959)

Haag (Jeannine S.) and Sullinger (Tami L.). "Is he or Isn't She? Transsexualism: Legal Impediments to Integrate a Product of Medical Definition and Technology," 21 <u>W.</u> <u>Law</u> <u>Journal</u> 342, 343, 347 (1982)

108

Hughes, "And Then There Were Two," 23 Hastings Law Journal 233 (1971

Hughes, "Married Women and the Name Game", 11 University of Richmond Law Review 121 (1976).

Johnson, Sharon "Changing Women's Names" The New York Times, June 28, 1983.

Loeb, David. Changing Your Name in California (Nolo Press, Ca.: 1979)

MacDougall, Priscilla. "The Right of Women to Determine Their Own Names Irrespective of Marital Status," 1 Family Law Reporter 4005 (1974)

MacDougall, Priscilla. "Women's, Men's, Children's Names: An Outline and Bibliography," 7 Family Law Reporter 4013 (1981)

Powell-Smith, Change of Name Problems, 116 New Law Journal 1027 (1966)

Right to Change One's Name, 5 Journal of Family Law 220 (1965)

Ross, Susan Deller and Barcher, Ann. The Rights of Women (Bantam Books: 1984), esp. pp.243-256.

Simmons, Change of Names, 113 Law Journal 212 (1963)

Status of Women, 20 Amer. Journal of Comparative Law (Fall 1972). The law in Great Britain, Sweden, Norway, France, Soviet Union, Israel, Senegal, which includes references to change of name.

Treece, Some Qualifications on Everyman's Absolute Right to Use His Own Name in Business, 46 Texas Law Review 436 (1968)

Women's Legal Defense Fund. Names and Name Change Information for Washington Area Women (D.C., MD, VA, 5th Edition), covers the substantive law of name changing for women in the three states, with basic instructions thereof for making the court petition.

CITATIONS OF SOME RELEVANT JUDICIAL DECISIONS *

In re: Anonymous, 293 N.Y.S. 834; 57 Misc. (2) 813, Civil Court, N.Y. County, Sept. 17, 1963.

Application of Lawrence (1975). 133 NJ Super 408, 337 A2d 49.

8 Cal. (2) 608, 67 p. (2) 94, and 35 Cal. App. (2) 723, 96 p. (2) 958. (Court approval of petitioner's name change application, on appeal, with the court reasoning that the court should pass upon the name change petitions more liberally since parties could just as easily have undertaken the change by "common usage".)

---

* Most were cited in the manual to illustrate various legal points and questions

Clinton v. Murrow, 220 Ark 337, 247 SW 2d 1015; Mark v. Kahn, 333 Mass 517, 131 NE 2d 758; Sobel v. Sobel, 46 NJ Super 284, 134 A2d 598. Cases that define the major issues and considerations for the court in granting or denying applications for change of a minor's name.

Flowers v. Cain, 218 Va. 234, 237 S.E. 2d 111 (1977). In the face of the natural father's objection to the changing of his children's names and the absence of 'substantial reasons' to warrant such a change (e.g., abandonment by the father of the natural ties ordinarily existing between parent and child, misconduct that would embarrass the children in the continued use of his name, proof that children will suffer substantial detriment in continued use of father's name, and the like), the change should not be ordered.

Fobush v. Wallace, 341 F. Supp. 317 (1971), affirmed 415 U.S. 970 (1972). The U.S. Supreme Court upheld the passing of court decisions in a few southern and border states, including Alabama, requiring a woman to use her husband's last name.

Hurta v. Hurta, 25 Wash. App. 95, 605 p. 2d 1278 (1979).

Jacobs v. Jacobs, 309 N.W. 2d 303 (Minn. 1981)

In re: Knight, 36 Colo. App. 187, 537 p. 2d 1085 (1975). Held that it is more advantageous to the state to have a statutory method of changing names followed, and hence, that application under the statute should be encouraged, and generally should be granted by the court unless it is made for a wrongful or fraudulent purpose.

A court should not deny the application for a change of name unless special circumstances or facts are found to exist - matters such as unworthy motive, the possibility of fraud on the public, the choice of name that is bizarre, unduly lengthy, ridiculous, or offensive to common decency and good taste, or if the interests of the wife or child of the applicant would be adversely affected thereby. And, even then, an evidentiary hearing must first be held before such a determination may be made as to whether 'good and sufficient' cause exists to warrant denying the application.

Krupa v. Green, 114 Ohio App. 497 112 N.E. 2d 616 (1961). In this case, the court, ruling on a taxpaper's suit to have the name of a married woman who was running for a local office taken off the ballot upon the claim that the name by which the woman registered was not her husband's name, refused to make such an order, and stated that: "It is only by custom, in English speaking countries, that a woman, upon marriage, adopts the surname of her husband in place of the surname of her father. The state of Ohio follows this custom but there exists no law compelling it…A wife may continue to use her maiden, married, or any other name she wishes to be known by…"

Laks v. Laks, 25 Ariz. App. 58, 540 p. 2d 1277 (1975). Divorced mother of three children to whom custody of the children had been awarded in divorce proceedings, had the burden of proving that children's best interest required that their surname be change from that of their father to hypothenated combination of surnames of mother and father.

In re: M.L.P., 621 S.W. 2d (Tex.Civ.App. 1981; concerns dispute over first and middle names only).

MO App. 527 SW 2d 402

Ogle v. Circuit Court, 10th (now 6th) Judicial Circuit (S.D.) NW 2d 621

In re: Schiffman, 28 Cal. 3d 640, 169 Cal. Rptr. 918, 620 p. 2d 579 (1980)

In re: Strikwerda, 220 S.E.2d 245 (1975). The Virginia Supreme Court, in the course of reversing a lower court's denial of two married women's petitions for name changes back to their maiden names, held that "under the common law, a person is free to adopt any name if it is not done for a fraudulent purpose or an infringement upon the rights of others."

APPENDIX F

ORDERING YOUR NAME CHANGE PROCEEDINGS
BLANK FORMS

For our readers' added convenience, the Do-It-Yourself Legal Publishers, the nation's original and leading self help law publisher, makes available to its readership a package of forms usable for standard name changing needs for most states.

(Customers: For your convenience, just make a photocopy of this page and send it along with your order. **All prices quoted here are subject to change without notice.**)

To: Do-It-Yourself Legal Publishers (Legal Forms Division) **60 Park Place, Newark, N.J. 07102**

Order Form

Please send me the publisher's standard "all-in-one" package of forms for name change petition filing, as follows:

[Prices: $19.50 per set of forms]

	Quantity (sets)	Price
New York's Name Change Package: For **Adult**? ☐ For **Minor**? ☐ •••	_____	$ _____
The All-State, all-in-one Name Change Package (national forms)		
For an **Adult**..	_____	_____
For a **Minor**	_____	_____

(Prices: $19.50 per set)

Subtotal..................................	_____
Postage @ $3.50 per set.............	_____
Sales Tax.............................	_____
Grand Total..........................	_____

Answer the following, by check off { ✓ }

	YES	NO
Party is married & will change family (last) name	☐	☐
Subject, Minor over 14, but below 18, is involved	☐	☐
Subject, Minor is <u>below</u> 14 years of age	☐	☐
Subject is Minor, other parent/guardian will give consent	☐	☐
I know the non-consenting parent's address, send NOTIFICATION form	☐	☐

Name of the city, county & State where you'll file: _____

I bought this book, or read, or learned about it, from this source (bookstore, library, medium): _____

_____

(Name & Address Please)

Enclosed is the sum of $_____ to cover the order, PLUS $3.50 per set for shipping, and local sales tax, as applicable.

Send the order to me:

Mr./Mrs./Ms./Dr. _____

Address: _____

City & State_____Zip_____ Tel.# (   )_____

* New Jersey residents please enclose 6% sales tax (approx. $1.17 per item).

IMPORTANT: Please do **NOT** rip out the page. Consider others! Just make a photocopy & send.

APPENDIX G

PUBLICATIONS FROM DO-IT-YOURSELF LEGAL PUBLISHERS/SELFHELPER LAW PRESS

The following is a list of publications from the Do-it-Yourself Legal Publishers/Selfhelper Law Press of America. (Customers: For your convenience, just make a photocopy of this page and send it along with your order. All prices quoted here are subject to change without notice.)

1. How To Draw Up Your Own Friendly Separation/Property Settlement Agreement With Your Spouse
2. Tenant Smart: How To Win Your Tenants' Legal Rights Without A Lawyer (New York Edition)
3. How To Probate & Settle An Estate Yourself Without The Lawyers' Fees ($35)
4. How To Adopt A Child Without A Lawyer
5. How To Form Your Own Profit/Non-Profit Corporation Without A Lawyer
6. How To Plan Your 'Total' Estate With A Will & Living Will, Without a Lawyer
7. How To Declare Your Personal Bankruptcy Without A Lawyer ($29)
8. How To Buy Or Sell Your Own Home Without A Lawyer or Broker ($29)
9. How To File For Chapter 11 Business Bankruptcy Without A Lawyer ($29)
10. How To Legally Beat The Traffic Ticket Without A Lawyer (forthcoming)
11. How To Settle Your Own Auto Accident Claims Without A Lawyer ($29)
12. How To Obtain Your U.S. Immigration Visa Without A Lawyer ($25)
13. How To Do Your Own Divorce Without A Lawyer [10 Regional State-Specific Volumes] ($35)
14. How To Legally Change Your Name Without A Lawyer ($25.95)
15. How To Properly Plan Your 'Total' Estate With A Living Trust, Without The Lawyers' Fees ($35)
16. Legally Protect Yourself In A Gay/Lesbian Or Non-Marital Relationship With A Cohabitation Agreement
17. Before You Say 'I do' In Marriage Or Co-Habitation, Here's How To First Protect Yourself Legally
18. The National Home Mortgage Escrow Audit Kit (forthcoming) ($15.95)

Prices: Each book, except for those specifically priced otherwise, costs $25, plus $4.00 per book for postage and handling. New Jersey residents please add 6% sales tax. **ALL PRICES ARE SUBJECT TO CHANGE WITHOUT NOTICE**

CUSTOMERS: Please make and send a zerox copy of this page with your orders)

ORDER FORM

TO: **Do-it-Yourself Legal Publishers**
   60 Park Place #1013, Newark, NJ 07102

Please send me the following:
1. _____ copies of _____
2. _____ copies of _____
3. _____ copies of _____
4. _____ copies of _____

Enclosed is the sum of $_____ to cover the order. *Mail my order to:*
Mr./Mrs.//Ms/Dr. _____
Address (include Zip Code please): _____
_____
Phone No. and area code: ( ) _____ Job: ( ) _____
*New Jersey residents enclose 6% sales tax.

IMPORTANT: Please do NOT rip out the page. Consider others! Just make a photocopy and send it.

Index